TEACHING MYSELF TO SEE

Before you start to read this book, take this moment to
think about making a donation to punctum books,
an independent non-profit press

@ https://punctumbooks.com/support

If you're reading the e-book, you can click on the image
below to go directly to our donations site. Any amount,
no matter the size, is appreciated and will help us to
keep our ship of fools afloat. Contributions from dedi-
cated readers will also help us to keep our commons
open and to cultivate new work that can't find a wel-
coming port elsewhere. Our adventure is not possible
without your support.

Vive la Open Access.

Fig. 1. Hieronymus Bosch, *Ship of Fools* (1490–1500)

First published in 2021 by 3Ecologies Books/Immediations, an imprint of punctum books.
https://punctumbooks.com

ISBN-13: 978-1-953035-32-5 (print)
ISBN-13: 978-1-953035-33-2 (ePDF)

DOI: 10.21983/P3.0303.1.00

LCCN: 2021931806
Library of Congress Cataloging Data is available from the Library of Congress

Book design: Vincent W.J. van Gerven Oei
Cover image: © Tod McLellan – From the series *Things Come Apart*
www.todmclellan.com

punctumbooks

spontaneous acts of scholarly combustion

HIC SVNT MONSTRA

Tito Mukhopadhyay

Teaching Myself
to See

Contents

One · 13
Joining Up Fragments · 15
Two · 21
Call that Hyper-vision · 23
Three · 27
I Believe I Saw · 29
Four · 35
I Saw a Story in the Sun · 37
Five · 43
That Darkness That I See... · 45
Six · 49
Erasing the Extras: Hypo-vision · 51
Seven · 57
Let Shadows Lead · 59
Eight · 63
...Where Seeing Isn't Enough · 65
Nine · 69
Cataloging Faces · 71
Ten · 77
Let the Flow Be · 79
Eleven · 85
There Is More to a Day · 87
Twelve · 93
Seeing through Smells and Sentiments... · 95
Thirteen · 103
Seeing Enough... · 105

Fourteen · *111*
The Half-seen · 113
Fifteen · *119*
Billboards! · 121

Afterword · 127

The Opulence of Vision

He still held on to his body
He just trimmed his sight —
Maybe out of necessity.

The frugality
of sight, sorting just black from white
simplified the body.

He wanted to carry
the weight of his vision — light,
out of necessity. Maybe

he ignored a "somebody" —
But that wasn't exactly the right
explanation! While floating, his body

acquires a visual simplicity.
Looking at people from a casual height
was the usual necessity,

World below looked liquid. He
wouldn't deny
that he still had his body
Escaping the opulence of vision — a necessity.

One

The airplane was passing through a turbulent area in the sky — who knows which part of the world it was? I did not make note of the date and time.

You remember details like flying, memorize the scratch marks on the airplane window and you never get to remember big details like the date. Time is a fuzzy logic in my calculations.

Details over details piled up in my mind — like those piled clouds clogging the plane and smearing the view. Outside the window a painter was covering the twitch on the lips of his portrait — first with a dab of white as if to forget the expression and then proceeded to erase the whole picture with manic whim, including her eyes. Sometimes you could see just the window and feel the shake of the seat, then hear the pilot's announcement without even bothering to follow up what his cracking voice instructed. All you know is that your seat is shaken somewhere on a wide cobble stoned cloudy road. Turbulences are no longer a surprise for me. I am desensitized through several years of flying.

As the clouds coiled a mesh around the plane, the pilot was boring tunnels and burrows to escape the entombment. Sometimes white blurry tentacles licked the window — so close to my face. Clouds probed inside — somewhere the erased portrait's eyes questioned those random strokes. There could be a desperate blindness in that seeing.

The plane was small and flying low hopping a "jiggety jig'"– like a random grass hopper. Bigger planes carrying many passengers fly really high to escape from the ground. Sky gets bluer high up there. Exhausting blue and blue! And you can leave your shadows down below all those ripples to forget them for a time being.

Inside this grasshopper's belly we wobbled on lumps and potholes — buckled and capsuled, settled to rattle. I looked through the window. One sits by windows to look through glass, and remember to see.

An abstract painting with smoky whiteness curdling thick and thin trapped my eyes. And flying was not supposed to be freeing the self! I was looking for anything like a shape or an outline to hold on to with my vision in that free form. My reflection through the window held me. Through the movement of the plane the faint shape of my reflection — ninety percent erased by the off whiteness, stared back at me like my free spirit flying in mid air — a fuzzy transparent visual familiarity parallel across me. At least there it was! I held on to it with my vision.

Someone could be painting the sky with frenzied strokes of whimsical clouds but forgot to erase my reflection.

Joining Up Fragments

What if I am a selectively visual person? What if I am seeing and yet I am not seeing you standing in front?

But I may see a bit of your shirt-collar and I may not see what you look like, because I can't escape looking at the shadow of your collar on your shirt. And then my eyes may try to look at your shoes, whether they are new and black. I prefer wearing black shoes. But to look at you, the all of you, your details, I need you to turn into a picture with a definite boundary, reduced in size. So give me your photograph and I will see you. The map is easier to handle than the wide spreadsheet of space.

If I have to make a list of what I see and what I don't see, there may be a pile of random things that may take up space here and I wouldn't have any explanation. To explain everything, one may risk making my "Autism" bright enough to see. Let the fog continue and let the search remain. But this is an essay on seeing pictures and understanding how to see.

I at least can see the details in a photograph! And I do see details of paintings or picture books on paintings as long as I can recognize the components that are painted. In fact, paintings help me modify my perception. I appreciate the concept of art to qualify myself in the world where art played an important role in the growth of human civilization. I appreciate the artist's eye, if the artist can explain how he is perceiving.

As far as I understand, artists can see more details that miss my eyes. When they paint those details, we all can find out what we missed in a real world.

There is this mist — its upward rise
Shapes, outlines crumble quietly as
Phantom details follow the eyes.

The artists create those spectacular shapes, sun over mountains, to let us explore every detail of the shadows that will linger on the painted foothills forever. And artists paint layers — color upon color, a hundred words of interpretation can grow out from those colors, spilling out narratives through frame and glass. Sometimes they would evolve in our heads as a poetry.

A painting can dig into the brain when understanding grows deep.

A painting can make a mystery that begins a terrific story.

A painting can scream with a voice. I can "hear" Edvard Munch's painting screaming out of the glass and frame. Edvard Munch punched the bones of being in his painting called *The Scream*. I learned that he painted it around the year 1893. The painting creates the orb of sound through the waves of black and orange, haunting the eyes. Today, when screaming is just a part of traffic and television sounds, road rage and politicians arguing, that solitary mask-like face in the painting screams out into modern times. Because you fail to understand why your eyes can hear the waves from the waving orange and the wobbling image of the terrified being of the painting, you wonder who can be the person whose orange black scream has intrigued the eyes through time. Because you wouldn't know, it can disturb your consciousness almost making you feel hopeless and guilty that there was the scream and no way to guess how the story ended. The painted scream evolves many possible stories.

Shattering the mist — was that a scream,
A cluttered language like a blasphemed
story, batting out from a guttered extreme?

The way I understand art is by heavily relying on the similarity of shape and color — either closer to the real shape or allowing some strategic alteration leading me towards the open door of hyperreality. Salvador Dalí's hyperreal clocks explode or crumble and hyperreal elephants walk on stilts on the canvas without being strands and patches of unreal vibes and throbs of whim. I can exist as one of his painted beings in the canvas and never be worried about the next security screening at the airport.

The way an artist sees the detailed lines of an apple, a subtle yellow line here and a faded red over there; the way he looks for the twinkle of light reflecting in a wee corner; the way the apple-bulge grows in the middle and narrows towards the base and the way all of that can be organized into the totality of a fruit would be represented on his canvas. That perfection which nature made a shape called apple turns into the immortal Apple-art by Mark Zelmer or Michelle Calkins. I can smell the apples in their paintings, feel their fresh and crunchy pulp. Yet some artists would want to distort the apple like patches of apple-like circles.

There will be a residual appleness in those paintings. I would conclude they are apples I am looking at through a thickened glazed glass. There would be a seventy percent chance of apple-like quality in those red patches.

My visual experience would have a delayed sensory feel; crunchy pulp would leave my mouth.

How far can the artist's take distort without destroying? I avoid going to modern art exhibits. If all the nuts and screws and bodies melt in a cauldron of a canvas how will I recognize a body? Even my selective vision can expect a head located above your shirt collar but there must at least be a head. I can expect your two eyes dropping their looks down at me. The temperature in those looks will let me know how abstract of an artwork I am! I can feel my curved image on your retina! But give me your photograph, if you want me to see how you look.

Modern art makes me feel foolish — especially when I stand staring at blurred red colors, dark red now, scarlet over there, a battlefield of color like exposed intestines, stating an abstract definition or representing an idea. Colors fly around in a space without bounded shape within the boundary of the canvas, and I am supposed to look at the caption *Summer Afternoon,* smoke fuming from fire in my brain from the caption. There is nothing to feel but see the smoke dissipate out of the chimney of my eyes. Holding on to the caption I search for the afternoon sky, my eyes suspended somewhere in the spaces of the painting.

And why wouldn't I hold on to the caption when all around me real colors throb in a blurred shapeless zone of red and green, blue or white, giving me no warning what their caption ought to be. And there could be your erased head talking through the sky.

Shapeless colors will escape like wild horses as I will hear the vibration of your voice; my vision will be a harness that lies idle in my head. Those trembling colors will wobble like an unknown fuming sea; my understanding, a confused compass. I will have no clue what to look at other than to catch hold of a caption. As if there is never a sun and never a shadow, just the caption.

How far can I pretend to understand?

Two

Everything grows outward.

It always clusters outside the tip of a pencil, molecule by molecule there is growth before it turns around — just to turn around and then turning tremendous with rules of photonics. Out of control!

Looking at all of that is a practice of the eyes.

Holding on to a pencil is the habit of my hands. Habit does not care about rules. Vision stops and eyes keep looking at the point of a pencil.

I like to keep a pencil close to me in case I feel compelled to write a word or two. There is no real reason to analyze why the word. Do not analyze the history of a blink or a casual staring at the tip of a pencil! I say do not worry too much to know the secrets that hold the tip of Autism. Over-analysis of a habit is a rule of Autism experts. You wouldn't dive with them inside that fluid unless you had something to hold onto.

The tip of a pencil with a bit of graphite can hold within its pointed space all the potential words you can think of! I can produce a whole book with that pencil point! You can follow the rules of language wringing out of it, then break the rules and in-vent a word and marvel at the potential! You might create. out of that pointed tip of a pencil, a simple Jabberwocky joke, or a whole homage to special education! Possibilities are endless.

Right now I am just hyper-visualizing the tip, learning how to look; concentrated world of language on that tip. Anytime there can be the Big Bang — molecules forming faces and windows or a wall scattered — and all beyond my control. I am not even looking at your face. Let the world explode!

There might be this centrifuge of layers, colors collecting and misfiring at nowhere and you haven't even understood how to look at a tip of a pencil.

How many times have you missed a drop of dew and later felt dry with sweeping guilt for missing out just because you were learning to look at a tip of a pencil?
Looking cannot be statistical.

My apologies if I could not find your face.
Looking cannot be free of guilt.

Call that Hyper-vision

Sometimes there is enough to see.
Sometimes it is enough to ignore.

Because I can focus only on one thing at a time, I often pick a point in space — could be an air molecule — and follow it around. I have no microscope in my iris to pin down a real air particle. Much of what I see takes place in my head as hyper-vision. As if the world is nothing beyond that point; as if the worries and anxieties of interacting with a visual world questioning my mind is out of question. The point grows conspicuous. Finally it is all there is to see.

The point sticks to the retina like a dart; and resistance is futile.

The point catches my eyes, vision gets busy in the field to toss the point around like a soccer ball; preoccupation grows large enough to blot a face, eclipse a body, then does more! A mountain vanishes.

The point is the resort where my eyes will reside whenever the world will be broken into many shapes — those jig-saw outlines of chairs, walls, picture frames, faces... and I will feel all the crumbling sounds from footsteps on wooden floor, pouring of water in a glass, jingling keys, voices that will blow a sound storm around my shadow.

The assurance of that point will blur the boldest shapes and outlines. It will hold my vision like a hand holding a hand and drag me out. I feel the shift. I always shift. The point and I will shift toward the nothingness of space. Sky is a mere limit.

I hold on to the speck.

Looking at space trying to picture a minute molecule of air — a speck of detached presence, unclogged by colors, I shift. Then I begin to move. Moving out, I blend all shapes into one final shape, then follow it around with my eyes to who knows where. Trying to search a destination for it, I may entrust myself a destiny of movement, as its faithful disciple, sometimes as its comrade. There is no need for words. I am a journeyman through the transparency of pure trust.

We move: the speck and me, together sometimes, bone to bone, the tibia — fibula, the next one to the next one. We move together, no reasons known, through the walls, through the moon. We float and drag. I can sink. It pulls me out, then I breathe again. And then it's the sky. Vision of the sky is best understood when we can isolate a speck of a star. I hold the pointed speck to scribble my journey.

The floor of sky, a spacey room,
The Milky Way — like sprinkled dust,
That no one remembers to broom.

I rise on the crests and fall in the troughs of what could be mountains of collective sound waves in air. I enter the world of swaying wilderness — the uncertain puzzle pieces of chairs and people, picture frame and social smiles. Sometimes tossed by a storm of a familiar voice I play like a raindrop; then let clouds scatter me around. Faces dissolve and blur in the frothing distance. Shifting the continents, I follow transparency. I move through swarms of

pilgrims around holy rivers, bazaars full of buzzing business, dust around those unpredictable feet, before I return to real shapes called tables, chairs and shelves, faces
and smiles blended in a transparency of pure trust. I trust
air. I hyper-visualize. But I cannot broom everything else.

Trust is unadulterated,
uncluttered air;
In an unbroomed sky of points.
Trust is knowing —
when there are stars
there would be space.

Trust is that wound you are bound to scratch. A would
like the tip of a point concentrates a tactile world. You do
not worry about summer or winter surrounding the skin.
But I must really be talking about seeing and not stray
away from the point.

One can follow an imaginary speck in the air, trusting
that there will be a return. I can travel the white ice-
smeared poles of this earth if necessary, sailing a solitary
ship — trust, without being lost, led by a mere point. I
can jump from one floe to another floe, a pilgrim of snow
carrying a flag to plant wherever the air molecule rests,
knowing for sure that even if my lungs failed, the molecule will continue to travel several centuries following
the Coriolis factor. Trust has nothing to do with what you
are trying to tell me while I move. Trust is the run for the
fierce extreme because there is a shield of safety called
escape. It is about ignoring puzzle pieces of doubt, then
again believing that an Autism organization will shine
the famous buildings blue once a year, trusting on a responsibility.

Hyper-vision lies in trusting the mind that is imagining
locomotion.

Imagination is fierce. It ignores unnecessary reasons. The speck in space will jump into shape as far as facts can be ignored. My pencil point will begin a point and scribble the equator's line with a long poem. And science is not even a matter to consider!

Then I will see it. Out of the blue, that speck will jump into existence as real as a blink, real as the diving of the moon all of a sudden to seal the sun during a total solar eclipse. Once revealed, it will out-shape all other shapes sealing the senses behind it. Perhaps those who see their God finds his presence thus. I just hyper-visualize the smallness around a pencil dot.

Call it hyper-vision. Call it unrealistic. I follow the gypsy air. Tomorrow my postal address is an "elsewhere."

How much of our lives are spent looking at the obvious? What is the world of vision but a clutter of shapes and structures, sizes, colors, stones and cobwebs, Meredith and Samuel's Facebook pages. Wave after wave they are seeking our attention, eroding the senses, numbing the pupil until all of it gets flooded with visual tides of exertion. We live tied up to a cluttered clumsiness, we forget to find the gypsy air. Why must I try and solve jigsaw puzzles with a million pieces?

I understand vision has rules. The simple purpose of vision is to navigate the surroundings.

How often do we break free of the visual obvious to find that floating absurdity and journey its path unbothered by the loads of visual rules?

Three

I always feel my temperature rise when I am looked at. A diagnosis of Autism entrusts one with a reasonable expectation of how others will respond to something unusual or out of the norm.

I live. And I offer visual interest around me. I believe that I have even become generous.... Everything — the morphogenesis of our cells dividing into heart and lungs, bones and skin, including our physical maturation and eventual decay — contributes to our beliefs. The chemical reaction in my brain from all of my seeing and being seen has taught me a vital truth. There is at least one predictable thing in the universe!

At times, I was a sacred map for a curious psychologist. He tried to discover a continent called Autism. He accepted whatever his textbooks told him.

At other times, I was an impenetrable fog for a stubborn therapist. He staggered his way through. A thick molecular jumble of vapor, I settled in his head. He believed that he could talk me to green and blue shapes.

Then, perhaps, I was a sturdy and impregnable wall for a special education teacher. He drew his educational graffiti all over me. He believed in a cause. I was the recipient of his beneficence.

While others formed opinions about what they saw, I swam through my days in search of my own beliefs. I had no need for science; I had a life to live. Why carry such a heavy backpack when air is already sitting on your head?

One day my belief tore the scaffolds through the crags and ridges of a brown rock. I could be crashing upon fire like temperature. I could feel the trap of temperature when I really began to look.

I Believe I Saw

If you see something being born in front of your eyes — like a piece of broken glass or perhaps a fallen leaf — and you let it grow old inside your head, then you can begin to believe what you saw. You may behold its shape talking to you. You could care less about its words — *what* it is saying. You believe you have heard this thing. And if you have heard it, you should have seen it. That is the religion — the temple, if you will — of optic nerves. Let me show you how I see.

I saw the brown rock — just by chance. Out of the plethora of things to see, it showed up in front of my eyes. Its color rested a little way from my foot. A brownish inertness, terrifically rough, as if the raw sincerity of blissful sleep had been preserved in its depths. When would it awaken and tell me the story of its galactic birth?

I memorized its shape. I memorized its color, as if I were encountering the object for the first time. There are so many shades of brown! Out of all the possible shades, *this* shade, *this* shape, out-shading and out-shaping the rest. My brain becomes an adoption center for such things.

The color wasn't just a smear at my feet. Pickled in a bottle of centuries, scattered all over the earth, assigned to the ground since the beginning of time, silicon and sodium and other elements gathering up equations in chemistry to sum themselves to — Brown! That chemical and mathematical Brown! Why do eyes neglect the brown earth so much?

Is it too practical in appearance, too obvious? Does it resemble the looks of a tired mother who bears plants, on which graze other animals? So many questions were blended in the outstanding shadows of that brown rock. Out of its cracks bloomed the colors of the world. Around it lay grains of dust that could be its eroded skin. And what about our skins? We are just fifty-one shades of brown in the name of race. Isn't the categorizing of skin absurd?

We live through absurdities. One day, our bones will turn to dust — calcium compounds and carbons, granulating — and we will each conclude the process of mastering what we see. The in-between is just a conventional journey of pupil and cornea through a colorful world. People look to understand. I was looking, but I wasn't understanding. Or, rather, a failure to immediately decipher my surroundings allowed me to see things in a different way. I was looking at the centuries hidden in the fractures of that rock.

Centuries turn. The brown shape continued to ripen. Time is a bottomless container. The bottom of the sea shouldn't be green as they show in National Geographic photographs. If exposed to sunlight, it would be brown.

Seeing isn't enough for me. I have to focus using subordinate senses. Sometimes I have to hear to see. Other times I must smell. I smelled the color brown as I breathed in the shape of the rock. It lay still like a dead civilization before me, a blind and mute presence of brown, bigger than the size of my brain. I was memorizing its smell, comparing it to its dark brown, deformed shadow. A sculptor might have seen a different shape hidden before scooping out the excess brown.

As if the rock were day-dreaming — as if it could see and hear its own ancient beginnings, which lay preserved within the chemicals that had determined its properties.
Cracked a million times by weather and rain and yet continuing to exist on the scattered soil.... Every particle of it was the continuation of a story that began somewhere in the womb of creation. Was it aware? Did it understand. Yes, it was, and, yes, it did.

Atomic sounds, the cracking of space,
An outburst! everything
as though out of place,
Churning outward —
a chaotic maze.

Because we possess language, we are determined to fuel our thoughts with it and state our opinions — those opinions fly like dust in between the boundary of earth and sky. Collective awareness floats as sound waves in air, interfering and dissipating. Sometimes thoughts stick around longer and form a memory. Awareness is forgetting to see the absurdity of everything. What are we doing measuring time, proving our positions?

What if there was no necessity to prove our position like that rock? What if there was simply the patience of eternal waiting and yet being aware of one's beginning? That waiting for nothing in particular within the brown womb of wisdom, letting everything emerge from it, including life, chemicals and language! Shaped from dust, we flatter ourselves with knowledge before returning to dust, in a cycle that continues. What if the rock was aware and silently memorizing my limited understanding of this absurdity?

So I let it grow in my head. I could learn to think like it and learn its patience.

What is alive and what isn't, who can think and who can't — these distinctions are taught to children in primary school. Doctors and psychologists told mother one day that I wouldn't think. Consciousness is determined by the presence of a brain. If you have a brain, a typical brain, you are capable of thought. No one has ever found the presence of a brain in foliage. Beyond the mechanics of photosynthesis, there is thus no consciousness or understanding the purpose of being. Yet the streptococcus will know out of survival instinct whom to attack without a mind or consciousness, not actually caring about the purpose of its being.

The rock solidified inside my head. Did it know that it solidified as the magma cooled? Beliefs grow solid as that rock, reluctant to change shape within the boundary. It took years to crack open the collective cranium and accept Copernicus. It will take years of weathering to crack the mind in a brown rock. I was merely nurturing its cracks. Cracks are required like human imperfection. What good is a psychologist's office without human imperfection?

All our two times two and definitions of photosynthesis, our political understanding and complaining cannot free us from the boundary of a dusty earth and so much brown of it. How did man react watching the brainless flu virus attack a DNA strand? The virus happened to navigate into a human cell without even possessing a brain to orient itself around the blood stream. Was there a belief working in that virus? Every scientist must learn to see its belief to inflict flu with or without a brain structure.

The rock in my head was the body of the beginning to complete my looking at the day.

The churning and churning, the in-between
The locking of eyes, the closing in
Thoughts must keep — spiraling.

Imagination is absurd and thoughts can create a fiction.

Four

It could be November or July; time is a fabric consisting of thread-like events. A big wide fabric, judged inferior by the picky perfectionist — thick here, thin there. Time weaves our day and night as the earth loops round the spindle called sun. One can see time flying away like a large handkerchief in the wind. But one must see it with something other than eyes: namely, the imagination.

I was sitting somewhere on someone's chair turning the pages of a magazine. And I absolutely don't happen to remember where. How I love to touch the glossy pages! I am the spindle and magazines revolve around me.

I flipped pages, over and over. Flipping through pages is a matter of choice. I was choosing to focus my attention on the feel of those pages — the equation of paper and skin left traces of my finger prints on their cool edges. People were near, with their randomly waving voices around my ears. I heard, but did not listen. There was no story in their talk.

The pictures in the magazine competed with each other — each one promising a story. Like an archeologist, I excavate stories. Then, I weave their scraps together. Weaving stories helps me to understand what my eyes won't tell me. Strands of vision must lead to a story. Otherwise they are just stray birds darting around without a branch to settle on.

Voices flitted above and beside me; the sun reflected on the glossy pages as I turned them. I grew my stories with those magazine advertisements.

I Saw a Story in the Sun

"The sun is a ball of golden strings, a ball rolling across the sky. Why wouldn't it roll? It needed to roll for the birds to play around it. The birds could then pull strands out from the sun to glow their nests at night. The miller's daughter weaves a ball of gold every evening, weaving the gold out of straw. She does it quietly lest someone discover her."

I used to make up stories about the sun. Stories are real when you see them with your head. Those stories un-story when reasoned with binoculars of science — weaving shards. You have two eyes that can stare at the blank face of air outside, but a hundred fancies are alive inside your mind — that is what you see when you see with your head.

A hint of a shoe from the Nike advertisement can create a story: "Once, a pair of perfect Nike shoes waited for the perfect feet. Then one day they were matched with two large feet with big toes. Little did the celebrity pair foresee the smell of stinking sweat as the glorified feet ran on a treadmill. They ran and ran — not going any further on the reeling path. How perfect could the outcome be?" Story spins around a picture, radiates questions — like planets around the sun. Then you begin to relate. Finally, you see.

It could be a ship — shaped as a cloud,
It could be a shape that was wiping out the mist,
If you still did not find a story in the shape,
It was never there for you.

I do not believe in reasoning as a clarifying force. My eyes need a story. Stories clarify everything that I see. And an absurd story is easier to remember. How many of us can remember realistic stories?

Too impossible to live without, stories light up a nest inside the darkest corner of my brain — inevitable as an egg, waiting to hatch.

While other children believed in homework and football, parties and taking tests, I grew my stories. Everyone must grow something. I had no homework, football, or parties because Autism closes doors. And yet, exactly as it closes doors, it opens a hundred windows made of stories to see through.

In what should one believe? That Autism needs a cure to un-Autism the mind? That getting straight As in school makes a superior student and a smarter being? That knowing how to swim can save you from a shark attack? That Facebook photos of an expensive vacation attest to a happy life? I needed believe in a story; my head can story anything! I can be awake in a story, hear people around — their ridiculous or serious conversations. I may continue that story, inserting the sun, the birds, and anything I can think of to complete the mixture of sensory jazz and imagination. Stories live in my head — they are as real as air. Blow away the air and nothing will change.

When I was little, I watched the story of light and shadows. In one version I saw the sun with grandchildren. Stop me if you can! People saw me but no one could guess which story had hatched. There was my shadow sketched on sunshine as clear and distinct as black upon white.

I admired my shadow under the sun's spectacular shine as I walked home from speech therapy in Mysore and Bangalore. To think about it, a story made of lustrous strings pulled out of the sun can actually confuse anyone who knows about the hydrogen—helium nonsense. Can your hydrogen and helium begin somewhere and end somewhere? Strings do! Even the tiniest strings can begin somewhere and end somewhere. Strings began stories — they began, they ended. Perhaps this wasn't reason enough at all for my stories about the sun and shadows. Perhaps I floated an absurd sun under which I walked home from my therapies. Still it was a wonder-sun! Still there were windows to look through.

I saw stories, as I see the arguing sparrows.

I wasn't old enough to reason. I wasn't young enough to forget the different shadows of myself shaping my beliefs. The world was fluid with floating solids that followed their shadows. I would rather dwell in my shadow than open my eyes to science. Wasn't the cause for Autism a shadow in real people's heads? Isn't there a big effort to cage that shadow for study and wipe it away?

One day, when the sun became just a chemical reaction between hydrogen and helium gases, I was devastated. Why does everything turn out to be something else? Even that breathing in and out you thought was life is merely gas and lungs. Don't count on it. The sun became the wrong kind of sun since then: its fleeting strings the strands of rays that a child learns to draw. The sun of my story was mere nuclear fusion. Shadows seemed beyond my hold.

It's a familiar problem. When little Johnnie realizes that Saint Nicholas is just the Bishop of Myra from the third century, he is crestfallen.

Everything, including my shadow underneath the sun, looked wrong after that. Daylight kept the earth wide awake, but daylight wasn't the sort of daylight I wanted. There weren't any strings in the sun. Stories melted in the pot called sun.

Just a little information and everything changes. Sunlight on windows and the reflections of trees through them were as bright as ever. My shadow and I continued to walk. I continued to look at other shadows, imagining whose shadows they might be, trying to find a beginning to a story that could end without the presence of strings. Who on a casual morning can pull a story out of the nuclear equation? I changed after that between yesterday and tomorrow, as if I had flown out of Moscow.

About five billion years ago, a cloud of gas and dust began to gravitate towards a center. It had a spin. Collapsing made the spinning faster as per science. Because the central region had the most material, density, and heat, it ignited a reaction. Light was born. Maybe the sun will never bother to remember the story of its own dark days.

Mother taught me how to draw and color the sun. I drew as many rays as possible around a circle that wasn't the sun. Strings of sun rays growing out of the circle, long enough to touch all of the tall buildings and all of the rooftops. The shadows of those buildings confirmed the presence of a sun.

Its light continued to illuminate my head and shoulders from outside when I walked underneath it. But the sun stopped hatching story eggs in my head.

The sun is a science story, one of a man gluing his eyes to a telescope. Joseph von Fraunhofer saw lines in the sun through a spectroscope. He was studying the spectrum of the sun just as Autism experts study the spectrum of Autism. The difference was that Fraunhofer had a spectroscope to see the solar spectrum whereas Autism experts have only their eyes.

Yes, only their eyes,
Which gives birth to a study.
After lengthy appointments,
My life has a label.

I heard details of my story from their reports many times. Fraunhofer found that out of two kinds of lines, the sun has absorption lines! People studying these lines can tell the history of the sun. I wonder how the spectral lines of Autism show up on the screen of an Autism expert's eyes. We don't get much, but we get a report that we are supposed to keep for the next appointment.

Science grows us. The sun grew with science. Autism can grow in numbers. And that becomes very scary. Be scared of yourself if you are Autistic — scared of your mind, your stories, your life. Even measles are safe! Be scared of your gluten, your ice cream that has dairy and of course be scared of your actions!

Perhaps when a Neanderthal saw the sun, he saw it as the shining eye of a giant blue animal whose blue skin covered everything above the earth; how this animal puffed out the smoke he saw as clouds; how it bellowed louder than a hundred lions when the smoke grew dark; how its forked lightning tongue licked away the distances before it was exhausted; and how when it cried, it wept rain. We would never know how he created ceremonies and sacrifices around the waking eye that rose up every morning and slid down every evening to sleep below the zenith of the horizon. Neanderthals did not talk or they may have. I have seen their skeletons at a museum. I wondered: could they grow stories without language if they did not have words — stories with fear, joy, and hunger — something worthwhile to believe? Language is nowhere as sophisticated as beliefs. How will you describe the taste of fear or the smell of sleep?

Without language to share a thought, each of us can hold stories of the sun within ourselves untouched by the views of science and opinions, untouched by the real photon impact from the gaseous star. Stories will have no basis, no spectrum.

Five

I needed to sniff the pages of my magazines. I always sniff pages — consider it a sensory requirement. The magazines were upstairs. I do not like placing them anywhere else. Hats have a place, shoes have a place, magazines have a place. Don't ask me why I do things in a certain way. Do you know why you need to drink that cup of coffee when you wake up?

I had almost learned to see the stairs in the dark by counting my footsteps, mastering the feel of the floor while I proceeded to calculate the sixty- or fifty-degree angles as I turned. The magazines would be upstairs.

I mastered measurements with my movements at night.

During the day, mathematics is out of my control. Numbers, during the day, are explosions of object counts and the business of the interacting world. How hot is it? Temperature will be a number in Fahrenheit. How smart are you? Your brain becomes a number designated by your IQ. How much do you know? Check the exam score.

Numbers become ridiculous extras for anyone who isn't interacting with the tens and totals of the purse and counts. I kept a count of footsteps at night, when numbers become quieter.

I felt the stairs while I climbed.

The one, two, three of the stairs — all to be measured and memorized.

Darkness would be thick and thin, cluttered or dimmed by the glimpses of sky through the blinds — light zeroed on the segments of stairs. Night could be the coal mine, I was the miner excavating my way. I did not need a Davis lamp. Night could be a black soup — I was dissolving like salt.

Night expanded exponentially beyond the walls, and I could be just a decimal point. Somewhere, there was the tictocking self measuring time in dark sounds. Programmed in its grooved gears, it unwinded the obsessions of seconds; I clocked myself in for the ritual.

If I happen to wake up at night, I need to sniff the pages of my magazines — one page at a time, all of them every time — and then to measure my steps back to sleep as long as I am not waking someone up. Rituals manifest. Rituals are the gears of Autism, grooved to rewind. Rituals bloom better at night. Don't ask me why. You are never asked why you drink your coffee.

Obsessions fade, other obsessions take shape, night returns mathematically in counts of hours.

That Darkness That I See...

I begin with darkness.
    In darkness one can learn to look.

The hotel room in which you are staying is a bowl of midnight. Perhaps a voice in a dream stirs the bowl to wake you up. The voice is strangely familiar, yet you don't know who it is. Some dreams dissolve like a puff of steam from a kettle. You may forget to guess what ingredients lie with you in that thick, black mess of a soup called night. Realization happens slowly, steadily. You are one of those erased by the darkness. You must learn to look at it.

You may be amazed by what you cannot see when you try to find the floor in the dark. Chairs and tables, walls and corners merge. Blackness smears. They conspire collectively; they want you to trip and bump your elbow — your eyes as useless as the expression of pain on your face. Can you really call it a mess when the hotel room was darkened by your own choice? Wasn't it you who shut the drapes before falling asleep?

Structures and shapes sit around like primordial beings in a state of incubation. How patiently they wait! How sudden is the pain! How patiently you forgive that corner of something that knocked your elbow or toe. Your eyes long to sleep again while the pain dissolves in the dark. Until then you wait for the morning wake-up call!

In the beginning there was only this patient waiting — until, until the first command: Let there be light. Is patience another name for darkness?

We are conceived in darkness; we wait to be born. One day, darkness will overtake us again, closing our eyes to death.

Patience in the name of darkness is primordial, older than light. Darkness has no speed. It is sloth as stability. It is a container holding the ingredients of every known thing. It is the background through which the light particle chariots travel at an assigned speed from the beginning of the "bang." Within darkness wait the energies of light and sound; waiting is all there is.

Rising from darkness of the womb at birth, sinking into the darkness of the tomb at death, all we get is the in-between allowance of light. How we celebrate the allowance walking away from the dark! How we forget that we are walking forward into the dark! How long is that allowance?

Experts recommend seven hours of sleep a day, seven hours to drown ourselves in darkness. That calculates to two thousand five hundred fifty hours of sleep or one hundred and six days of sleep in a year! In twenty-five years an average human being shuts his eyes to darkness for seven long years at the recommendations of doctors. Giraffes are different. On average a giraffe will sleep for just five minutes a day!

That's all.

So much information related to sleep, wakefulness, intensities of light, the blackness of black holes.... So little allowance of life! How much of the weight of information can a brain bear?

Darkness churns up millions of lights; churns out the brilliance of galaxies.

Universes waiting to be born from impenetrable black holes, strong enough to twist anything that dares to approach its blinding reach and tremendous gravity. Theories of science, of life and death, facts and philosophies — all churn inside that unknown according to laws we do not understand. Our ignorance is that darkness. Information is born from it. And what could God be doing while everything waits to be born? She imagines. She thinks.

Darkness is knowledge.
    You just bring it to light. An encyclopedia can only reach the eyes when you light up the pages.

If light is the clutter of color waves, then will the merging into shadows unclutter everything? Darkness isn't the mess; darkness is the cleanup, sweeping vision into the oneness of a single vibration. So, let the cleanup begin. Let the differences in human color cleanse the clutter of racial difference. Let all black and white and yellow and brown people stand in darkness and be the one color of solidarity. Darkness will enlighten the mind. Let black matter, let brown matter and let white — o everlasting white — matter subside. Maybe even being Autistic will matter as well and not be shamed into a disease.

Light is everywhere in space. Between the sun and our earth there is light. Yet space discards light perhaps by choice, discards dense matter, but allows its passage so

TEACHING MYSELF TO SEE

that the first air molecule in the atmosphere can absorb the sunlight and begin to scatter and stir up the morning sky into pure blue. Day breaks. Light breaks up the red from the green, isolates the tables and walls, everything that darkness assembled. Darkness is ubiquitous even inside our occipital cortex while it makes sense of light.

Space is content with miles and miles of darkness. For it is not the light that we see but its stimulating effect on matter — it's what makes us see the red and green of a tree and the many greens of a field here on earth. Blood that pours out as red flows dark within our deeper bodies. Space in its bigger darkness holds the brightest of the suns and dullest of the planets like a primordial mother who will never let go, whose face is beyond our imagination. That darkness that we call the unknown is what lights all of the lights.

While I scribble my words — black marks of letters on the white paper — I learn the thoughts of my mind. I cannot understand the whiteness of this page, but I can bloom my mind with those dark, graphite words. So let me learn to look at darkness.

Six

"I have never seen those people in my life."

"But they are our neighbors."

"I just cannot remember seeing any one of them. But I re-member many shoes by the door. Too many shoes. I remember taking my shoes off, too."

Years ago, I was in India and had this conversation with mother. I used to "hand write" my conversations ,since my speech seemed to be dissolved in my bones or perhaps my liver. There come some social hurdles when one is anointed with Autism. Some of us — "the chosen ones" — do not speak as a social expectation. We face a cave, our backs to the social light called speech when we reply through our bones. I better start writing, or you won't learn anything from me.

In India, footwear is supposed to be left outside at a designated place away from the living area of a home. If you wear the shoes on the streets, then they can't be invited in. The rule is universal: family and guests, all leave their shoes outside. No exception.

I was visiting a neighbor for some function and had followed this social rule. As usual, mother had returned home with a bag of questions for me when I walked out after spending just five minutes inside. I was too young to answer the details of the whats and whys. So mother had to re-word the questions to discover what I saw and heard and what could make me walk out. Mother followed me. I knew my way back home. It was two houses away.

"You found the right pair of shoes. You did not pick any random pair."

"I have never seen those people in my life. But if there were shoes, there must have been people." My reply was final. "If there were voices, there must have been people. And the ceiling fan wasn't moving."

I do not know what more I could have answered. I had seen a bit but not a blink more. I refused to spill my sensory plate with an extreme load. Visual stimuli are like salespeople. Everything in a social gathering is for visual sale. People clothe themselves to stand out; places are decorated to make them look out of place; faces smile at each other — the smiles are enhanced; the smiles seem to expand out of, and away from, the jaws that make them possible. Every smile expects a reciprocal something.

That's when I hypo-visualize; that's when I reject the capitalist solicitor called visual stimulation. One doesn't have to answer every YOU'VE-JUST-WON-A-VACATION-IN-ARUBA-OR-HONOLULU phone call. One needn't adopt a Disney World-like sensation to arouse the eyes.

Vision for me is more than enough. A profligate enhancer. Do not be intimidated by its wild proposals. Like a nagging salesman, your vision will sell you every corner of the galaxy or glare, or a glorious smile and expect you to pay for it. Vision has a radical scheme followed by the principles of manipulative capitalism.

Erasing the Extras: Hypo-vision

Vision is a long ruler with two ends. Call one end hyper-vision; the other, hypo-vision. There is my seeing — my looking from this end of the ruler or that.

Looking is like drinking. You can look as if drinking with thirst or you can look as if drinking without thirst. If you look for the beyond when you are looking at space filled with air, imbibing deeply what you are looking at, tasting the possible events around a single speck, you are hyper-visualizing. You get the tingle of the tangy taste.

But if you look at everything and there is no hunt in your search, if you let the deer and ducks glide away, surrounding and dissolving through your eyes like salt in a solution, if you merely taste the insipid crowd of shapes and colors, then you are definitely hypo-visualizing. I hypo-visualize sometimes. I am the drowsy lion letting the mice play by my feet, breaking the rules of Aesop's fables.

When I hypo-visualize, you may move an elephant around me and it will dissolve in the sky. Just like that. "How many fingers did I show you?" you will ask and I will tell you "sixty-five — maybe." Nothing is incorrect in the scale of counting details. I break the rules of counting when I hypo-visualize.

When details are erased, simplifying the vision,
Shadows evaporate into insignificance,
And light is merely a process of liquidation.
Don't ask me who you are — don't ask a question.

The world will remain the "world"; your face will remain
your face — always filled with visual details. And yet I will
have no clue whose face you carry. Don't blame my social
skills. What I happen to see is not exactly what I am supposed to be seeing. I am expected to see much more. Yet
I hypo-visualize, no matter what, if vision tastes insipid
in my mouth. There is no point in drinking any of it. I
will be that Aesop's crow forgetting to put pebbles inside
the pitcher to raise the level and drink. I will forget that
I am thirsty.

"More" is just a word when things crowd around like com-
peting stallions, ready and alive to dart into the retina
cracking open the cornea to find that feeble optic nerve.
The brain is just a poor grazing zone because there are too
many grazing thoughts nibbling around.

Then comes the part of selection — which stallion en-
ters first! Allow them in — but one at a time. You will see
that door hinge. But you may forget about looking at the
door. You study its brass shine and the reflection through
that polished surface and equate the world outside with
the world inside that reflective yellow polish. You situ-
ate yourself as a balancing factor between the objective
world and a kind of imaginary one. You are lost in one
thought: what would the outside world be like when
looked at from within that convex reflecting surface of
the brass door hinge?

Like a Big Bang, the world grows out of the convex
focus of its brass curvature. Like a Big Shrink, the world
shrinks inside it. You have forgotten to mark your eyes

in that mix up. What's the point of vision without the mark?

The only stallion that could graze the mind so far has eaten up all your grass. You did not even know what the other stallions were like. You depend on a mere belief: if there is a reflection within the door hinge, there ought to be the door! And included within that belief, the world where you are standing is a blurred concoction.

You churn out a concoction, breath becomes a rhythm,
Exhaling time, "shifting across a digital chasm,"
Molecular moments crumble — atom after atom.

As far as I know, the world of space, color, and size, what typical eyes enjoy seeing most of the time, is too massive — it's like an overloaded suitcase; every random picture is akin to Fourth of July fireworks. Where will you turn your head? One has to leave out some of it. I leave out everything. The ruptured bag of sight can be left out in the junkyard.

Stephen Wiltshire never leaves out a line. Stephen Wiltshire is an Autistic artist who can ride on a helicopter around a city and draw the entire city by memorizing every wall and dome. I marveled at photographs of his drawings. I, too, have seen the earth from the sky during many of my airplane trips. But I could never memorize the many shapes below me. Cities and roads, lines and domes evaporate. The sensory feel of movement remains as a thick precipitate for me to taste. Does Stephen Wiltshire get a chance to hypo-visualize in private? Could he blur those walls and domes of his drawings and see through the very core of earth?

I am aware that I am not seeing enough — that I'm no Stephen Wiltshire. I see melting shapes, leaving out just a few of strands of lines to enter my pupils. Who knows what has entered and what has not throughout the years! Ask me what the man was wearing or what sort of picture was on that wall, and I can excuse myself by replying, "I don't remember." I can't explain why there was just a line from a shirt collar or the outline of a picture frame on something that could be a wall.

To understand what was recently around me, I depend solely on photographs — those compressed images of the external world, shrunk by scale, to know *which* man, *which* picture. I can dive into the two dimensional depths of that flattened photograph and see myself in it, staring at the door hinge in the corner. I can be a minute Flat-lander who lives in a rectangular space, stored away in an envelope.

Imagine the shock: a whole person, a whole wall behind that person, and then a whole background behind that wall are, in fact, a street and a world? Without their photographic representation, they just evaporate. I exhale them and eventually erase them out of sight, as if they had never existed. I hold on to a belief called existence and laugh at the absurdity of your disappearing shadow.

Is "a person" the same as "could be a person"? There is always a step-by-step process around his erasing away — the ritualistic erasing of eyes and then the rest.
    The something called a wall, too, has a procedure to complete its disappearance. I try very hard not to erase those shadows.

How will you describe my belief?

The word "belief" limits our vision. Our visions are influenced by what we are taught to believe. It restrains us. You cannot cancel a belief with just a thought! If there is a body, there must be a face. If there is a face, there are bound to be eyes blinking. There is only one way to stop their gaze. Ignore the body — even if the shoes are bright yellow. You may follow a rule: erase the eyes first.

Call it hypo-vision. Hypo-vision happens like a riddle to be solved. A flash of green and yellow, smile and shadow, and perhaps a sudden darting blue moving towards a red chair. Your eyes hold onto the chair handle and let the erasing begin. There is vaporization beyond the chair.

Everyone knows the rules of seeing. We must see to survive. We must see to appreciate. We must see to differentiate. I know the rules. Learning the rules of seeing and breaking them is a kind of art. Picasso would like it. Wasn't it he who said, "Learn the rules like a pro so that you can break them as an artist"? Hypo-vision is an art.

To live in the world as Picasso would draw it — managing the simplest of lines, wobbling and dripping faces blurring into one another (who a face and what a face?) — can definitely add up to the art of living. Life, like a schooner, has to navigate anyway, and blending the solids can create enough fluidity for the ship to move, as the real world darts around the eyes like excited sharks. Hypo-vision is the boat that can enable you to cross the tide and find the coast without drowning in the sea. Row the sea and race ashore to escape the terrible sirens of vision.

Nick Bostrom, professor of philosophy at Oxford University, proposed an unusual question. What if we — our looks, our likes, our thoughts and emotions — are all holographic images borne of a super computer's programming? We live within a simulation, see what we need to see. We are here living this pretend reality.

Shakespeare understood this idea. He included it in his play *As You Like It,* with the famous line "All the world's a stage, And all the men and women merely players." It's not easy to accept, but understanding it is sufficient.

What if the rules of seeing are part of that program? The sunset is simply solar radiation caused by the rotation of earth as we are moving away from it. Remove the program, and the world begins to evaporate. There is no world in coma sleep. Even that chair evaporates. A nullified brain gets washed by cerebrospinal fluid. The EEG will show five cycles per second. The shop is closed to dream.

Why not hypo-visualize when I am not yet dreaming?

Seven

Like a will-less shape, I was gliding on the expansive parking lot surface, scavenging for shadows. The parking lots of grocery stores are always punctuated by pigeons. Their shadows light up my vision.

The mind answers to no one, strays by itself,
like winged shadows on gray
cement. The waxen sky melts.
What do those shadows have to say?

Pigeons fear nothing. Not even a crumb escapes their beaks — even if it lies inches from your feet. Each parking space a platter of plenty. My feast is what the light does to their search for food.

The mind floats all by itself,
listening to their feet. Ears rebel.
Language vaporizes, compels
pigeon-steps. A pigeon self?

The Greyhound bus had made a brief stop on its trip to Dallas. "Ten minutes of fresh air or picking up snacks from the grocery store at Buda," the driver said. Getting off the bus was a choice, and every passenger opted for it. I knew why I was climbing out. I had to follow the dance of lazy afternoon light as it spread

*across that Texan flatness like a dazzling haze — frank and up-
front.*

The mind answers to no one — least of all itself!
The parking lot: a white, wax-filled tray.
On a July afternoon, the lone star swells.
Here and there, wandering patches of gray.

*I had no immediate need to look anywhere. The airborne pi-
geons, with smudged outlines, circled around the grounded ones,
who walked clearly. Pigeons prefer to walk. I could hear sounds
in their shadowed feet. Everything else had a skin of light.*

Let Shadows Lead

Another afternoon in July.

The sun shone that day, too. The buildings seemed to scribble their shadows on the pavement. I was in a car moving across the light. My own dark shadow was moving with me.

Shadows are darkest when sunlight is brightest.

Charcoal patches below everything moving or static under the sky.

Through the glass window, in the mirrors, I saw a world dripping with colors grounded in their shadowy grip. I saw these colors on cement, on grass, as traffic signals materialized and dissipated — a rhythm ushering me away and into their waves or ripples. I rose; I plunged. Waves of streets moved through my body; the world emerged and escaped — an armada of fleeting colors. Buildings were ships at anchor on a sea or mirage of light, anchored by the rims of shadows.

I was the stick-man of a science diagram talking about wave-lengths and frequencies attached to the sun. I was linked to it with its own steady flowing light waves. As if the world were just a page and anyone could stare at it. My brain broiled, my thoughts smoked, my imagination spilled frothing. My shadow was a black hole to gravitate me towards escape.

I could be a puppet. A puppeteer could be moving my hands and cooking my thoughts under some bigger plan. A grand puppet master called Sun pulled the string-like waves whenever he wished to change the shape of my shadow. It was utterly elastic: my shadow could stretch and shrink more than my actual bones and skin.

The July sun in Texas has a tactile intent: it wants to touch everything it sees. The July sun that day had a dispute with the clouds over sharing space in the sky. It knocked away all the feeble clouds that tried to patch shadows on parched patches of ground. July sunshine has the darkest shadows.

Let me tell you about shadows. There's more to say.

Shadows become my visual destiny when the sun throbs closer to my head, like a glowing heart. It loves to melt that scented candle that you placed some time ago and forgot to carry inside. Was that a pumpkin-scented candle?

I was inside a moving car that day, teaching my eyes to look beyond mere shadow. I was learning to admire its neatly done outline — as if a giant pair of scissors had snapped the light strings around it to create its distinct borders.

It lay, half on the seat and half on the floor to my left side, faithfully waiting for me to wave my arm. It turned with the turns of the car. I was waiting for the luminous puppet master to tug the strings so that I could wave at it. The architect of shade is always the light.

While teaching my eyes to understand my shadow, while urging my eyes to look around for any waves outlining it, I was learning once again how to un-detail the world. There are just too many details under the sun! Un-detailing is zeroing out all of the visual load you have to deal with — and there are many of them! You say there are two apples? Place their shadows under my shadow. There will be zero apple-shadow. Shadows will blur your best mathematics.

To un-detail a face, when faces are just compositions of skin around the eyes, nose and mouth, one has to subtract many factors. When you un-detail a face, you must subtract the name of the face-bearer; you must eliminate unnecessary activities such as labeling a face as pretty, ugly, bored, excited, sleepy, or worried; you should not feel pressure to finalize whether the face is familiar or unfamiliar, or could be familiar. You just subtract everything out and leave the essential human shape.

Shadows teach me subtraction without numbers. With the shadow of a visually impaired person or a hearing impaired person, I will subtract the impaired part along with many other details, yet still let it exist in a flattened shape. Talk about eliminating Autism! It isn't a science project, however. You must simply look at the shadow. Looking at the shadow will let you subtract the medical terminologies and still keep the human being intact.

No matter how you look, every flattened patch of a person called shadow will blossom under light, mathematically squeezing out the details. Removing details, shadows leave a residue that is neither matter nor energy. Einstein wouldn't have found them worthy of the energy–matter relationship.

Shadows teach me how to add. When my shadow spreads on a table, the table stops being a table. It becomes something more. I have seen shadows float on water and sink in water, ignoring the laws of floatation. And shadows pattern the walls, yet remain unclogged by the extravaganza of colors. It is a mad-holy vision.

Shadows do not differentiate. They form a perfect equation. A king will have the same property in his shadow as a beggar. The pride and prestige of the king are just a patch in a shadow. Even the eager expectation in the beggar's expression wouldn't be allowed in the general rule of the stoic shadow. We are all equals — socialism in shadow!

Pick a round pebble and pick a gold coin. Shadows will not give a dime.
    Living, non-living — every entity has a right to at least a shadow. If anything is democratic and non-judgmental, it is the shadow, that ancient philosopher of democracy.

Shadows have contributed to the light of my education. I remember my mother teaching me how to trace my shadows when I was learning to hold the pencil to write. Because I had good visual attention towards this thing, I was motivated to trace the outlines — shadow of a ball, a hand, a rectangular page or a ruler on the cement floor when she held them high against the light, long before I learned to write the curving C and O or the hard straight lines of K and N. That was years ago. Those shadowed days of my childhood froth and spill.

My shadow sat idle, yet it had an outline. It was a faceless shape, shifting with the orientation of the car. I cannot remember where I was going that day. When I see shadows, I let them pull me with them, shape me up, lead me on.

Eight

I follow a tradition. Call it a ritual and it won't flatter me less. The life of an Autistic pilgrim is a three-way shame:

1. *I never clutter my visual bag. I see what I need to scavenge, scavenge what I happen to be hungry for. The visual tourist takes in what the guidebook dictates and discards the rest. I, however, taste the insipid and yet feel visually full. At the restaurant called My Surroundings, I won't order the eyeballs' appetizers. Nor will I order dessert.*

2. *I never let my eyes work alone, because I do this thing called sight with my other senses: touch, hearing, and smell. It's a collaborative affair — boisterous and chaotic. My eyes share the responsibility. Think of it as a kind of government, a rickety system of checks and balances. Let every branch do its part.*

3. *I am never without questions as I meander through time. The "what" of sight often eludes me. My vision erodes as much as it identifies. It's like a river in a storm. "What could that be that just washed away?" I've stopped looking back — there's no point. The questions accumulate; the objects escape.*

...Where Seeing Isn't Enough

The Pilgrim of Walmart! The immense parking lot has a special texture, a matted finish that you can almost touch with your eyes. Adding to it is a kind of a cement smell — not so much dust-like as beyond dust-like, akin to lingering sunlight or perhaps rain water stroked by wind. Smell it with your eyes, only your eyes. Because we never seem to find a parking space close to the entrance, we must walk and walk. And I must smell and go through the revision of smell every time. What cement fecundity! It's our weekly, not yearly, Pilgrimage.

A thousand cars could fit in this marvelous holy land. The shopping carts would park themselves if they were allowed. Picture them standing side by side, brotherly shoulder to brotherly shoulder. And still there would be room for Black Friday shoppers! Of course, the wind would send the carts careening into one another and into their metallic brethren. Pity the brake-deprived! Beware the owner of the manly truck or suburban minivan! These are no-nonsense people. They all voted for the stimulus and health care in 2008, and they are determined to buy their super-sized soda from the McDonald's outlet inside. With insurance for all, who needs health food?

I see Walmart with a sort of pride — there's no pretense. It's pure democracy. As someone Autistic, I usually stand apart; here I'm included. Thank God for ordinary Walmart! I look forward to walking through the lurid aisles and to drinking up the magnetic discord. I look forward to taking in the many smiles, to feeling the warmth of my brotherly walk with my cart. Even my Autism looks perfect under the thousand fluorescent lights whenever a toothy grin approaches and fades. I thrive in the ordinary, and no one weeds me apart.

Our Walmart! It can be yours too, if you care to enjoy touching what you see. It can be as simple as a potato in the vegetable aisle, as common as a jacket in the clothing section. Try it on and put it back, then see more, touch more. Pick up the packet of socks. Sniff it if you want, abandon it you don't want. Move on! There are plenty of things to do in Walmart, and no one is supervising. You know you won't buy these goods, but you touch them all the same. You touch what you see. Nobody minds. Everyone touches things at Walmart. Go ahead!

I have seen Black Friday shopping at Walmart on television. Recently, I saw a glimpse of a baby in a stroller. I named it Carlos Frederico José DeSilva. Two months old perhaps, Carlos Frederico José DeSilva shopped for the first time half asleep in his stroller. He was perhaps the youngest shopper. The local news channel was reporting a fight over a television set. It was all about — who touched it first? Vini — vidi — touchy... and claim! Then fight to conquer.

I imagined Carlos Frederico José DeSilva watching this scene for the first time, receiving an education in complex socially interactive vocabulary. His sleepy eyes open like automatic garage doors, as he closely watches the contest for the thirty-two-inch television set. Did someone forget about his stroller, in the rage of the race? Carlos Frederico José DeSilva wouldn't find it worth remembering who finally won the TV set, yet he did get to watch the little argument that happened around it. Two people touched it first. Is that possible? Someone saw someone else touching it first while someone else also saw someone else touching it first, too! Perhaps he was learning from his stroller that Walmart is about touching. People who heard the swearing of undocumented vocabulary flowed in from all directions, like the confluence of many meandering rivers, emptying the shelves of electronic items on their way. The television showed a smartphone video of a self-declared bystander. Some people just like to watch and won't offer help to anyone screaming their tonsils out.

To make the most of what you see at Walmart, you must touch. But during Black Fridays, to make the most of what you see, you must empty the shelves. YouTube always memorializes this ritual with poorly taken cellphone videos. We need, after all, to celebrate human potential!

Though I poke fun at television touchers, I like standing and watching the TV sets in Walmart. They play identical programs from their designated places. A whole wall is given over to them. For a while, you forget that your purpose is to touch things on the shelves, so long do you stare at these indistinguishable soldiers. The TV sets might as well be marching in North Korea! So what if you look and look until you begin to believe that you must tele-fill your living room wall?

No one will stop you. Go ahead and look. Go ahead and erode time with the wind and water of your vision. Green will look greener. The TVs at Walmart are neon celebrities compared to the one you have at home.

We Walmart shoppers plough through the Walmart, loading up our king-sized carts with artificial potatoes and artificial apples, artificial bed sheets and artificial undershirts. We feel ourselves fortunately organic. Others like us plough right alongside. "We who ain't reading labels, ain't affected by the fear of bird flu in Timbuktu." We know how to smell the glare of lights, we know we can touch the yellow jackets made in Vietnam. We are tribal.

We've seen those health-food stores. They look like another world, a strange place resembling the surface of Venus. Their shopping carts are like space probes for the informed food shoppers who are scared to die. You and I, the common people, will buy food for survival without scrutinizing the number of calories and carbs. We who are pilgrims know how to float and bloat inside the bigness of Walmart. We nod and shake our heads whenever there is a health-care debate. And we boldly go back with not a centimeter worth of doubt.

There is more than seeing — at Walmart. You learn to see and not to stare at an isolated being who perhaps wants to touch each item from one end of the shelf to another end.
   No one will isolate him.

He is just a common body like them.

Nine

I am fixated with a particular picture in a National Geographic magazine. The picture is that of a face, which I am yet to memorize — colors splashed on a page; ink and print on glossy paper creating her contours. I would rather stick to the ripples of her story and wait for her face to float.

Her face is liquid; the refugee girl's real face in that picture never solidifies.

The magazine is two years old now. Magazines tell their stories, yet never complete them. I just recognize her staring out from the page.

Her fixed staring at the camera horrifies me — I have memorized her staring without an image of her face. There is no future in the stare. A page full of a face, dissolved in the smell of paper swallowed by a stare! Her after-story grows like bubbles that she had perhaps breathed when the camera clicked: "How she finally escapes the glistening page, the magazine smell, the disgrace of being a refugee; even animals know where they belong! How she finally becomes a real face, forehead filled with dust." — I have made several versions of her story.

I own that magazine. And I go back to that page to read my unwritten after-story many times through the week! Pages smell different with years. Stories are retold, every time revised, never repeated.

Dogs love to play, cats can do their thing, but a photographer's camera will capture one face after another to trap in a page.

Most faces have common stories. That commonness fills the background like living protoplasm; then suddenly out of the deep pool of commonness, one face stands out, you see an awesome face-story in the social wave. Sometimes you trap the face in different senses to remember it — almost like the unique library codes they had in the British Council Library in Bangalore. Doesn't matter who the face belongs to. You know the code like a password, in that hard drive of your head.

Cataloging Faces

Who knows how others remember faces but I do it this way.... Sometimes a story will help me catalog a face.

Eyeballs ripen like pods. Will they rupture?
Outlines of people like clouds keep sailing
Scrambled faces — mixed together.

Recognizing faces could be an incredible ability. People don't talk about it taking it for granted. As if they will never realize how much struggle it is for someone like me. Perhaps they are not willing to know, how I have to go further down the road to fiercely fish the faces lurking underneath the surface of a social sea.

I encounter faces all the time — at the airports, planes, and random stores. Every encounter needs a tremendous visual and social stamina. But I must explain how important memorizing the face is! Otherwise what is a face but just a sitting scaffold around its story? But storying all the faces is beyond what time will allow. I can make one story at a time.

Creating a face story is one way, however time-consuming it may be to memorize a face in the social sea of scrambled faces. This face story is not what the camera is showing. I create them. I create face stories about how the face escapes the photograph and prints, leaving a blank space on the page so that I can write that story. Face stories enhance the face to bring out the visually hidden aspects. How will the camera make a story? I have imagined face stories in photographs of smiling faces even though they are not blinking.

I had once created a story of a stern-faced statue in front of a college — its bronze eyes looking with a metallic indifference radiating earth smells. My story was about how the face would look wearing a mask of a superman to humor the camera lenses; and I had once seen a face story without a presence of a face — in a sky full of smeared clouds making an artwork like a child's face painting. There was once half a face on the bare branches of a tree whose huge frowns and wrinkles grew outward from those claw-like twigs one October. There was a possible face, once, in the shadow of a lamp post stretching across the ground continuing into a brick wall. Faces lurk in those unusual heres or the usual theres. Faces don't have to be human. Please don't trap a face on a skull! Let a story grow the face.

Once I also discovered a face in a camel. It was chewing something, indifferent to the ground and dust, standing under the shade a few years ago when I visited a country called Bahrain. There was an awesome story dropping on sand from the drool.

A story in a face is found either sedimented or swimming underneath it, or it is elusive like an evaporating and dissipating mist. But you would hardly miss it, even if it left the face all alone stranded with mere looks and a smile or a shadow under the chin. Once the story is gone the face is just any high-definition looks until that face begins to talk. Only if I hear you talk, I will know who you are, by matching your familiar voice upon your stored voice. Shape over shape, your voice will be the fingerprint in my brain simply because I rely more on my auditory sense than visual. So don't just smile at me. Talk.

Occipital explosion — camera does not capture,
I recognize voices — outlines could be sinking,
Isolating voices my senses don't rupture.

Last week I wrote a story of a face in my head. It was a heavily made-up face of a flight attendant of the last flight—JFK to Austin. There was a story masking a tired face underneath the artificial eyelashes. She asked what I needed to drink. Her story had the smell of hand wash and the feel of leather armrest; it had the weight of a long day. The story floated around the seats like a boat, floating over the flow of the airplane sound. I asked for apple juice. I have formed a habit of drinking apple juice on the plane. But this was my face story fished from air. "I named her Clara. Clara wanted to be home and yet she wasn't. She was serving me apple juice. Smiling was her job."

I am a story hunter. I do harpoon stories, especially out of faces. Once I even peered inside a handbag of an assistant-teacher to find a *Vogue* magazine where a picture of a muscle man on the cover stared out at me — with a fist-sized face and furrowing frown. It was only a face. The assistant-teacher had snatched the hand bag out of my homo-Autistic reach. Hunting out a face story necessitates facing risks. His story begins like this: "That muscle man got stuck to a magazine page trapped in the bag of an assistant-teacher. He had no way to discover how the special needs classroom teacher would require a Vogue magazine and impart a special education to her trophy students."

Swelling clouds made of faces gather,
If I had sky poles, I could start them a-swaying,
Separating voices from that scrambled mixture.

Perhaps the habit began as early as childhood when look-ing at shadows felt less miserable than the contours of a face. But how many people actually remember when hab-its glue onto them?

The process of a hunt may be equal to tedious: tracing out the shadow of a person, imagining the three-dimensional head, then concluding an approximate face and finally figuring out the story takes up a complete day. Small hab-its go a long way if you manage to hold onto them. Did you ever imagine that if our shadows held our faces hos-tage, how in the world could we recover them?

Photographs of people helps manage the facial details. They are stuck to the page and wouldn't blink to distract. Harvesting out a story in a face of a stranger's photo-graph is a cultivated skill.

Shattering eyeballs split with pressure,
Vision enhanced I watch them sinking,
Rupturing nerves sink them deeper.

Autistic students are told to grow social skills. Face rec-ognition is the key to the social doorway — and I am right on track. Any Autism expert ought to give me a high five for that.

But sometimes stories don't grow. Ideas don't rain enough in the brain farm. I need assistance.

I allow the other sensory channels to assist me, help me catalog storyless faces. I can attach a face through a sim-ple sound of splashing water or a combination of smells from page 29 of *Illustrated History of the Sun* and the over-cooked potato. Call that synesthesia where senses blend without hesitation, or call that coding. I am not even interested your sciencing up of a holy process. I see an unlimited possibility that senses can offer in this coding process. It is by taste that we detect the presence of salt in a glass of clear water. It is by the smell of air freshener that I can detect that I am inside the belly of JFK airport.

Some faces can dissolve like salt within that massive sea of face solution. You swim and the brine washes your eyes. My senses rescue me like the Carpathia saving the Titanic victims in the sea. "What is that smiling face looking at me for? Aha! That is Carlos. I can smell dampness of rain full of sentiments."

Emotions from faces start raining all over
Wind turns wild as my hands keep flapping,
Without a flagpole I can't separate the mixture.

Habits grow me. The more I try coding faces, the busier is my nose — inhaling the smell from a book or a magazine or a candle trying to get a perfect attachment — the right key for the right lock, the right nut for the bolt, the right sweetness for tea, the right sort of right for the left. So every time I would smell page number 63 of *Where History Was Made,* I would harpoon that blotched face I saw at Walmart. I had named her Rosali. I usually siphon out a smell inherent to a page that I would assign to a face. What a gift!

Faces clutter, emotions rain heavier,
Sea full of their eyes around me floating,
My ruptured eyeballs drown deeper,
I hear their gurgles mixed with my laughter.

Others may work it out differently. But let them come forth and explain!

Ten

I am a part of the flow....

When I try to fit myself into the bucket of humanity, I always spill. Like an unsettled definition, I shape myself watery. Forget what the experts say about Autism; their knowledge is anything but solid. Autism flows: it doesn't settle; it doesn't shape.

Sometimes I see the reflections of a shape called "window" and a line called "wall," but my watery spread doesn't define anything. I wait to evaporate. The elusive air sweeps over me, and I continue to disappear in a molecular wind. Yet I return back to the flow. I return to spill once more.

When was it? It could have been last year, or the year before, or the 1990s. A bleached Indian summer sky waited for the monsoons. "Rice costs more when the monsoons are late." That was what the shopkeeper had told mother in Bangalore.

I saw myself as a molecule of water licked up by a cloud. I floated around, becoming the atmosphere. Who knows how.... I would drop back to the earth in a bucket. With great effort, I remembered my liquid looks that resembled humankind. I saw myself in a vapory presence floating like steam above the smell of hot rice.

The dead will forget those whom they loved. But water remembers the years of waiting. So I spill with my watery memories.

Let the Flow Be

Everyone waited for the monsoons that year. And everyone was glad to see them go. The fields were saturated. Rain had poured down for days in buckets, emptying the sky. Mother had placed a bucket under the dripping ceiling. The landlord promised to repair the ceiling after the monsoons. No one works under the pouring rain.

Clouds born again
Sky — their sagging cradle,
Mist curtained,
the sonorous drizzle

Sagging clouds swung the cradle.
Something almost said
to a metallic town in silver drizzle,
"The light looks dead!"

Something almost said —
houses listened; cars blurred
with powdery rain. "The shops looked dead!"
The smudged outlines of headlights shimmered.

Floating on reflections, cars blurred,
The clouds and streets refracted.
Shimmering lampposts silvered,
Visually displaced.

One can never get used to looking enough at water — whether it is coming out of a faucet like a thick
transparent line or it is dropping from the sky, drop after
drop. The line seems to link the sky and ground. Imagine millions of water faucets turning your vision wild! It
requires skill to stare at that illuminated transparency.
When you first look at it, for instance, you can't see a
thing except a rushing flow. Then it becomes a belief. The
basic religion of existence of life on earth is water. Even
an atheist believes in it.

You look at the continuous movement until you begin to
see more. What you see is just the fragment of an immense continuum, molecule after molecule. A journey
through time, a vigor emerging from the faucet, or a
steady point on the spread of the cloud, flowing wherever
the flow takes it. You see a rushing stamina, you see a perpetual cycle of life; and you forget to compare it with the
fragile mortality trickling inside your feeble veins. How
old is that drop of water you will drink?

Raindrops used to be as simple as millions of frantic water faucets. The vision of raindrops improved when you
read somewhere that they are spherical and not at all like
liquid pears or tear drops that the picture books show.
You read the details — how they begin as a sphere, with 2.7
millimeters in diameter, and gain weight, as they drop to
5.8 millimeters in diameter, shaped like a bun. The larger
ones can grow as big as 7 millimeters in diameter! That
big? Some even form a little constriction in the middle
and rip apart into twin droplets, while they drop without
caring where they are dropping so long as they are falling

somewhere. Your eyes had taught you to see them wrong. You used to see them too simply.

A child, I understand, looks at water in his innocence, understanding words like "flow," "damp," and "dry," "clean and wash," "drink," "swim," "splash," and "waste." When I was eight, I understood flowing water differently.

We lived then in Bangalore. How old was I? And what is age other than a flow of experience filling up a bucket of life? Like some of my neighbors living in the low budget area of the city, we had no running water at home. Although there was one water faucet upstairs, the pressure wasn't sufficient for where we lived. We had to collect water from a common place downstairs where other women lined up their jugs and buckets. I followed mother to the common water faucet, to queue up our buckets for washing and cooking and bathing — we had four plastic buckets in all but we made several trips. I wasn't supposed to touch the green one with a lid. That was the water for cooking.

The neighborhood water faucet had rules. There must be a queue. Mother had two hands for two buckets to pull water upstairs where we lived. So we made several trips. I was supposed to follow her up and down. I associated water with lines. Lined-up buckets, lined-up stairs — climbing up and climbing down again. It all seemed to be a kind of flow, water spilling as we climbed and vanishing under a mop. Clouds flowed in, smearing the sky as a viscous gray paint, layering on more of viscous gray. Mother carried one bucket at a time because the other hand held the black umbrella. I had to wait inside standing on the steps while she went down. We did not have that long clothesline then to dry wet clothes. I needed to stay dry.

Coming to America was like an entitlement of water faucets. Suddenly there were all of these water faucets under my control. So how would my looking at water flowing down the faucet be different? I still prefer filling up a glass full of water from a common faucet and drinking over those water bottles. I still look at big swimming pools as huge buckets that can save someone labor for several days — the answer to the long queues. I could never step into a pool of precious water. I saw hundreds of thirsty buckets in the chlorinated pools. How divided the economics of water can be! How united the water is that flows through those oceans!

Coming to Austin, learning about the city's fast growth, adding to the population, I thought Austin was a bucket. People flowing down faucets — the Bergstorm Airport pouring people in, pouring them down I-35, gushing them out of Greyhound buses, down into minivans and those U-Haul trucks, moving people in. All of this filling up Austin. The city population has grown almost twenty percent in the past ten years, me being one of the many drops. By the year 2040 there will be an added five hundred thousand people. Then everyone will be under Stage Two water restrictions during summer. We'll all live in newly constructed apartments and watch a drying yard. Construction is everywhere. A "one-day-a-week watering plan" for your plants may not be a greenery solution but at least it will be something more than a drop. The city will have to come up with an approach as to how to divide water between humans and plants. How does water divide? It won't be as easy as ten divided by two.

I saw people flowing on the evening news.

Refugees poured into Europe. Europe seemed a little bucket, refugees tributary-ing from the Middle East. Political questions from authorities like valves controlling the flow, humanitarian hearts puncturing the valves as the Middle East emptied out its citizens. Whatever you may believe about this matter, it doesn't affect the flow. The valves have turned out to be weaker than what authorities want them to be. Waves of people with viscous desperation spilled over country after country.

Yet oddly this is supposed to be a story about looking at flowing water and not drifting back and forth in a highway of time. To understand anything, we must go back to the beginning. "Water in the universe was first produced in star formations." That's what the Nova program specialist was telling. "The outward wind of dust and gas created the environment in which molecules of water could form; molecule after molecule joined forces and floated around, finding its way across light years to flow on the earth and eventually become oceans!" And how do the clouds draw water from those seas and oceans that harvest those tremendous living seals and whales within their massive depths? Water is a belief and those atheist dolphins can swear by it.

Water molecules trekked down to earth through space, still flowing perhaps in frozen clusters, entering as giant clouds, their blurring of stars and sun, gray-white to gray, curdling the skies. They rained over a lifeless earth to cycle through centuries, their sculpting out edges of mountains, deep terrains, gorges, and large meadows until the starfish began to breathe. What I see as water flowing out of a faucet is just a fragment of many rains, many snow storms, melting, freezing, flooding, and evaporating, daily rising up tides under a moon in a perpetual cycle of existence.

Let there be a unified belief in flow.

Eleven

I was touring the British museum like an aimless whale in the sea of a suppressed din, now plunging at a corridor, now emerging in the hall of war paintings, now lapsing in a room with ancient coins, and now surfacing again in a room with stately statues. Broken heads and arms solidified the days of distance. Waves of energetic tourists wandered around me, through the long corridors with labeled artifacts, when I suddenly woke up in the room of the dead.

The emperors of Egypt lay there, as real as daydreams. I had never imagined seeing so many of these dead bodies, so close and so harshly lit up under their glass cases. My history text books show only one of them as though it was lying alone on a solitary altar reserved for the king, posing for a photo-shoot. I woke up facing their metallic faces, which had been reduced to mere skull and skin blackened with time.

The chamber was large. The mummies were well preserved — they were not on altars but within glass cases on the platformed floor. Big sarcophagi stood as decorations, with wide-open covers that released their carbon-altered kings to the long fluorescent lights and exposed them to the nightmares of Osiris. I stared through the glass — as from the other side of life.

I had dreamed about coming face-to-face with a pharaoh, and all at once I wake up to a room full of them — frozen rag-wrapped, like untidy parcels. Do I even remember what else I saw before or after? I vaguely remember those marble statues and perhaps some copper coins — or were they bronze?.... Everything uprooted from its doom in some other display emporiums.

How intentional are daydreams? Someone hauled me out and floated me right on the surface, face-to-face with Egyptian blue-blooded personalities who once built those geometric wonders for the ever-after! What of their own daydreams? After all, they ordered slaves to place stones in such a way as to perfect the angles of their pyramids — only to have them looted in the future.

There Is More to a Day

Daydreaming differs from selective, hyper-visual seeing. While hyper-vision enhances what lies before the eye, daydreaming is the voluntarily created story — the manufacturing of images in the mind.

The fertile farm of the mind is more than enough for planting dreams. Grow that pyramid or grow your script or grow both. Your mind is as secure as a Swiss bank safe. Your daydream will not be hacked by any hacker. Its images will not be discovered.

A daydream, although invisible to others, becomes your reality if you can surround yourself with seeing like a holographic movie theater. You draw new boundaries to cross the limits of seeing. And soon the day isn't enough.

So go ahead — fish out that Goodwill job coach from last year's November right in front of you in that daydream. You may even paint a red mustache on his face as part of the hologram. He was assigned to be your job coach. And he followed you with yelling and tantrums in impatient gibberish, just because you did not have the right motor movements to do whatever he was yelling about. You heard his frustration at being insufficiently compensated for the toughest job in the world: job-coaching. "One of these days...." You had walked out of that job, determined to end the new language and his woe. You never saw his real face. You gave him a face in a daydream later.

Faces turn out to be more real in daydreams. Just as your education outside of the bonds of a "system" turned out to be real within a special-needs bracket. When someone talks about finishing school or college, I feel surprised.

Did you learn how to be misunderstood? My learning it was real.

Did your college teach you how to conceal your cogitation within the volcanic space of your mind? Did you learn how to be rejected? I learned. And did you learn to laugh and to see the whole system of existence as a simple joke?

Or did you learn how to be bored? People get so panicked about retirement and being bottled up. What will they do after retiring? As if a "job" is the only way to survive. I can give a whole lecture on how not to do anything and survive just fine — by daydreaming. I can create a whole college course on this.

Sweeping away the clutter of a situation as with a giant mop, replacing all needless stimulation, your daydream will decorate your mind with its own artful fancy. At first your breath and your body reside in both landscapes — the real one that you mop and the replaced fancy that you intend to enter and decorate. In the beginning you may stand at the threshold of the two worlds — the "here-and-now-world" against the "could also be" world — in utter confusion; then you decide where to step. Your stepping is clean. There will be no clutter. Sounds will be erased as walls begin to whisper.

You prefer to hear them whisper at you. You prefer any gibberish story to a job-coaching yell. Like gibberish graffiti making a point, your story will begin to whisper a new script. Yelling faces will squeak, and the mustache you drew on that face will start fading on one side till you make the face actually "talk"!

You know, and only you know that this world of daydream is real and that you are unlimited. I like unlimited freedom! I am a disaster with mathematics — but I can explain how to get unlimited wrong answers. There is a restricted rule of writing the correct answer and there, on the other side, is the freedom to give any random answer to seven times five. You can feel free to write six plus six equals a cross-eyed kangaroo.

There is only one right answer for your test. But wrong answers? I have a million choices and can care less about that big failing mark that someone will give me on a test. Did you learn how to give a wrong answer and still feel good? Feel really good?

Colors are brighter here when you paint that face green or greenish-blue... unlimited choices! The job coach will let you do that in your daydream. A splash of green to fill the space of his open mouth will quiet it.

Some daydreams are less intense.

One day, while daydreaming, I had been memorizing a vague impression of a man standing at a bus stop on Santa Monica Boulevard; and I had just seen Los Angeles for the first time! This was long ago, before the bus rides had turned ritualistic. I had just seen the darkest shadows of people and seagulls on the sandy beach right across the bus stop; I knew that I was definitely coming back the next day to see more of those dark shadows.

I knew I was supposed to look at the sea like everyone else. But I cannot remember whether I even saw half of anything called sea that day. I just saw outlines of people walking and the dynamic calligraphy of shadows on sand. No one knew what gibberish was moving around on a page called sand. In the daydream I invented a language and a script with those shadows.

The man at the bus stop continued to be just an outline. His shadow on the cement pavement was a dark brush-stroke. I had daydreamed a story — in my new language.

We went to Santa Monica to see the stores, the beach, the people. We were learning how to look at California. We did not know that day that we would end up staying in Los Angeles for three years. The man whose outline I had memorized never showed up again. Once, in my daydream, I finally heard his shadow talk. I read aloud the heading to my story translated as "Singularity."

Looking at the wall, learning how to day dream, you can teach the shadow on a wall how to talk in your language....

Life goes on everywhere, breath after breath, meal after meal, ritual after ritual. Everything follows like faithful domesticated animals in our minds. You couldn't count how many more memories your brain can keep track of. They will pile up as you try to remember that particular day when you saw a creeping ant by your foot that ignored you because your face didn't matter to an ant. You had to imagine its thoughts in an ant language — something like, "Where is that dead beetle they were talking about?" It had crawled outside your shadow limits. Daydreaming about it allowed you to memorize the ant's thoughts.

You have created many real memories of daydreaming in your mind. The memory of a daydream may matter more than one work day at the Goodwill store! And the Goodwill store's good job coach will give you a lifetime's worth of rent as he lives inside your head. You may grow your lifetime's worth of interest from that rent he pays just by daydreaming. Fair and square....

And I daydream about the refugees. Moving is a part of life when you become a refugee. Perhaps cameras and words don't matter. They will put your face up on a page and leave you with your dark shadow. You understand life like air and smoke, like evaporation and explosion. You understand dust and you know everyone is dragging shadows. Sun swirls, shadows change. You memorize the weight of a bleached sky. Within and without you imagination is starving. Your questioning eyes look at the photographer's camera. You have memorized stories that are too real to remember, too much like gibberish to language them. Even at night you could be up with a daydream.

A daydream is more than just a real ripple on the stretch of dust, or a shimmering mirage at the end of the horizon. Look at that wall to your side, for instance. Freedom can be created with just a scratch of an imaginary green marker. Then inventing new shapes, designating them under a new geometry, calling them by new names, you become the daydreaming Euclid, lassoing those wild amorphous scribbles, finding a reason to assemble them as a structure. In one of your daydreams you co-author the *Elements* with Euclid, the father of geometry, by looking at that wall where Euclid's shapes and measures merge with all the amorphous shapes of shadows creating one fuzzy singularity.

Thoughts are vulnerable. Imagination has a will. You can plant a shadow even on the sun's face, then dream up something and store it as a memory. One day you will write that book proposal recalling each daydream and no one will believe you. No one needs to believe a super-dream.

Like boys on roller skates, day dreams ride thoughts. Like new islands they show up and vanish beneath the waves, and no one can know what you are listening to. A familiar voice bubbles and pops between here and now, mountains float, dunes vanish.

The refugees don't go to any promised land they dreamed of all night! They just pile up their shadows under the plastic tents. Their tents are like a patchwork quilt on the rocks and sand. Settle here or there watching a photographer escape like a stray strand of cloud, taking away their pictures. Life was about watching everything ebb and wane. There couldn't be a place for a butterfly anywhere on dust.

Pharaohs see the land of Osiris in a hall full of museum visitors. And a young parent sees Abolishing Autism in the April fund-raising parade.

Daydreams of a future cure keep them walking.

Twelve

Smell matters! It enhances the visual image. I remember the image from one afternoon. And I cannot ignore the memory of a smell!

The man had entered the McDonald's while we were in. He had a relaxed walk, that of a king who was disguised in a tattered dress. He knew he was following some kind of a philosophy, proving a point. As if his disguise was what he was trying to communicate, underneath it there was his evacuation plan — a secret experiment on society.

Immediately the dining space emptied all by itself — quietly. Such was the turbulence in the air molecules! People rushed out like fish escaping the trap back into the sea gasping for the street's polluted air! The smell of fries that one can smell outside from the parking or sometimes a mile away from McDonald's was immediately replaced by the smell that he had brought in. The king wasn't in any rush. He came with his invisible broom. Before he left slowly, he did not forget his refill of the large cup full of Diet Pepsi — his experiment on society was done and complete. The sound of ice, the gurgle of liquid and then the quiet desolation of the empty chairs winked at him. Probably he will return again later to prove a point.

Why don't countries use an army of people who refuse to bathe to win battles instead of using all that expensive ammunition? Use a man who has farmed a field of bacteria and still walks like a king, a philosopher working in his brain. Diogenes once told Alexander, "Stand out of my sunlight," when the king asked the philosopher who chose to live on the streets what he can do for him.

How many people will offer a soap bar instead of walking away from his light?

Seeing through Smells and Sentiments...

You may blend your senses with my senses here to understand this part....

You could be going through rain sitting in a Greyhound bus. A high-school student could have calculated a formula and theory around the relative movement of the bus and your being stationary. No matter what you and the bus are going through, you smell the inside of the airtight bus. Buses smell different when they travel though rain. Nobody calculates smell.

There is rain before your eyes and the color around you is no different from the sky. Every car passing by is a shred of reddish or a blackish streak of involvement, as though interrupting the otherwise gray space. The overall color of gray simplifies the visually complicated earth in the rain. You are not quite interested in outlines. You are forced to smell the seats and the confined space. You contemplate and discover a formula for smell.

Two cars on the other lane — shreds of interruptions, then their blending sounds a big swoosh and then the swallowing. The sound of rain swallows the swoosh;

somewhere an occasional honking; drivers must see through swoosh and slush! Far away, a deep rumble from the intestines of the clouds. There could be a radio announcement, warning about the flash flooding somewhere inside a car. Our bus rips the liquid gray and moves through — with some mechanical formula in the intestines of the engines. The solid world of outlines is just another joke when the rains pour thick! You realize you are the guts of the bus digesting the visual watering. There is this strange smell. A semi-wet jacket hangs from the seat in front of you. You can see a head sprinkled with hair. Smell is a neglected mathematics.

You will be farther from a town when the bus sloshes fast.

You may even try looking at darker points — it could be a refraction of a bird or a distant house, and if you are looking carefully, you could also find a slender tree floating between the spaces, now erasing, now gasping, then drowning until you have moved a mile away from it. The Greyhound bus window is not the same as the Hubble telescope, isolating star from star. The Hubble has no clue about the different smells that could be out there.

Rain in Texas does not believe in any equation for the eyes. And you are just smelling through sights creating an experience valued by sentiments of a random memory. Your limbic system uprooted them randomly. Somewhere in the street food stall of Bangalore, the smell of roasted corn sharpened the prick of the drizzle. The man had squeezed lime and sprinkled a drizzle of salt and pepper. You remember the charred smell under his big umbrella. You recall a shower curtain at a hotel smelling of hotel shampoo. Texas is a tub too big to believe in shower curtains.

Our left eye is supposed to be separated by its identical twin, the right eye, by a distance of fifty to seventy millimeters. There is a slight difference in the coordinates of an object seen from the left point of view and the right point of view. But thankfully there is the brain to smooth the binocular disparity, helping us to recognize the depth and distance of those dots and lines, blurs and angles! The equation lies in the recognition, how the dots are joined. If a small blur is a bird against the wind, and a bigger blur is a rain-washed house, what will you call a slightly darker blur that is thicker than a tree trunk and is swaying on the road side? You saw it through the smell of the hanging jacket swaying with the movement. It isn't going anywhere. Why is the nose placed halfway between the eyes? Doesn't the smell of the dangling jacket remind you of an armadillo? Just from the distance?

Once you saw the body of a dead armadillo on a trail. Its strong decomposing smell spread throughout the area. The laws of smell, like light, like sound, spread with a Doppler ferocity through a field. There was a dampness in the air and the smell seemed to thicken a brew consuming the trees or even the bicyclists who whooshed passed whiffing the wind. The body of the armadillo — greenbacked and white-stomached, scales and claws, was the only thing that seemed to matter on the trail. You were looking at a still picture uprooted from a picture book you possessed long ago in your childhood that happened to mention "A for Armadillo" instead of the generic "A for Ant." You have never seen a living armadillo but have memorized the green and white stillness of a dead one. It wasn't raining that day like now while your bus moved.

There was no rain to wipe away the world that day. Erasing the road and trees, the armadillo's green back and white stomach was too alive in the smell. Life wasn't being balanced by the living green decay from millions of feeding bacteria and the fading of drying Texas grass. Green wasn't balancing either with the browned grass. Even the sunlight was just a porous presence seen through the smell.

Armadillos have a strong sense of smell and can smell up to twenty centimeters below the ground. The smell of the dead armadillo had followed you home making you wonder about the potentials in the energy of decay. Life begins with reactions, ends with reactions; all along our "living it through" and "dying it through," we are doing nothing but balancing equations as we metabolize, as we see and hear. Seeing through a smell is just a matter of balancing another equation. Biologists memorize life and decay, diagrams and equations. Someone will see through the proto-ness in the protoplasm and discover what primitive plasma smelled like one day. You were merely recalling the smell of decaying protoplasm in the armadillo and now its memory returned in your jacket. That jacket would complete the journey to Dallas with you.

You could be seeing through smell. So blend your senses with mine.

I can find the exact light switch without faltering at night in my room because I can see through smelling as I get closer to the switches. Smelling in darkness is not echo-location. That's for a bat. A bat will depend on sound to see. As a bat depends on sound to see, I depend on smell. The light switch is closer to the sink. The sink smells of hand soap.

Many times I can even harpoon out the white curtain swaying under the ceiling fan in one of those rooms that I used to spend time in, while growing up in India through the sea of distance. I have the memory of the wet earth smelling from monsoon showers that blew inside through the window — the wet earth smell intensifying near that window. Sometimes there was the smell of carbolic acid that was sprayed around the house to drive away the snakes if they decided to be a guest, because their homes would be flooded with rain water.

Smells from memories will roll in with the tide every time I see the rain. Darkness may pool the world, gray may flood the eyes, but I will fish up a smell from any sea.

One day, I fancied looking at a broken porcelain tea cup on a window somewhere. I had isolated it out from this world and placed it on the altar of another world that lives inside my head. I had given it a voice. I had named it Prometheus. Prometheus had no smell, but Prometheus was accommodating. It just blended with the smell of candles or whatever was around it. There is a responsibility when we place an object of interest in our minds. We have to keep it alive by mental movements and activities. And you may be surprised how much seeing through one must do in order to keep a broken porcelain tea cup alive inside one's head without a definite smell! Imagination is a kind of parallel seeing without the actual visual input. But it is undoubtedly seeing through. I have recalled Prometheus through all kinds of smells of curry and pickles, candles and tea.

Seeing imagery requires you to bore a hole and puncture the phenomenal world into a hyper-visual zone where you are the master of the light and darkness. You can even float that psychologist's head like a bloated moon and puncture it with a pin! Wasn't he describing you without bothering to plug your ears first? All you did was smell his glass door, instead of approaching him like an obedient service dog when he called your name. You did not even bother to explain him that if you don't even smell the glass you may miss out a bigger picture — how it mists up from your breath!

I think I was given a diagnosis once again that day for not responding. He was happy enough to understand that not responding balances an equation of not knowing. Everyone has to balance things up!

Seeing through reality is like digging a canal to irrigate a field of productive wonders. You grow, you harvest. You are the master. Grow whatever you want. Grow that smell from a broken cup.

Stuart Cumberland saw through his blindfold and found hidden objects. Stuart Cumberland picked up a subject's hand, saw their thoughts, spoke their thoughts back at them. Stuart Cumberland wouldn't claim to be telepathic but in fact disputed the concept of telepathy with the Society of Psychical Research, because Stuart Cumberland found a way to see a thought by feeling the muscles of a person. Stuart Cumberland died in 1922 without teaching anyone how to see through muscle movements of hands. And Stuart Cumberland left the medical doctors with nothing but an X-ray machine to see mere bones through muscles.

On the first day of September, I tried seeing through the mirror in a new way — the parallels, the contours of my face, the left side turning right. We were in harmony. We copied each other like synchronized dancers. The seeing had no smell.

On the second day of September, I saw through my image and noticed how irrelevant the position of my heart is. There was no smell. My nose was up there.

On the third day of this September, I saw through my image and realized that I cannot know enough. Did that image learn to read a book from left to right? The details of the laws of reflection, the lateral inversion of images, may just be mere explanations of what we don't understand. How relevant is our understanding against our image? I would never know whether my image smelled like my aftershave. Did it get the diagnosis?

Even doctors provide explanations when things get out of control! When a patient's medical condition is beyond control, doctors call it Autism or Bench syndrome or Bingologism. Medical books are full of names and examples. Explanations and labels can hide much of their cluelessness. And who has enough time to see through a smell? That's why I urge you to blend with my senses.

Churchill once said, "If you are going through hell keep going." The man will keep going without a shower, going back to the McDonald's for refills, defending himself from rain and soap or sponge, blow-drying the dining space clean of people.

We wouldn't even know all his secret thoughts. But we saw him smile his indifference like Diogenes, chuckle with the ice cubes.

Like Diogenes of Sinope, who was revered by Alexander the Great, who ridiculed Plato yet managed to leave his wealthy home and settle in the streets, live in a barrel, and refuse to bathe, the man pushed the boundaries of human tolerance.

He started the new school of thinking called "Cynicism."

I thought this man was collecting something through his defiant indifference. If given a chance, he was ready to teach something big, as if a modern-day Diogenes were visiting the materialistic world. Perhaps he would wait till the right moment comes.

TEACHING MYSELF TO SEE

Alexander said after meeting the wise man on the street, "If I were not Alexander, then I should wish to be Diogenes."

Thirteen

There is something dazzling and radioactive... in his beingness. The man — he could be me — refuses to blend with the humans around him. His beingness radiates a thing called Autism!

He doesn't know where he carries it, but he must carry something. Otherwise, why would people gawk at him?

If you carry Autism, you better do your Autism right!

Many people will look at you; a curtain of preexisting beliefs will prevail between you and them. Movies and books about Autistic individuals are like swatches at a fabric store — so many designs to choose from! Are you doing your "Autism" right?

Even if you are standing in a remote corner of a room filled with an impervious crowd, you will undoubtedly be seen through. You are like radiation from a nuclear particle, undaunted by the barricades of humanity, detected by "eye" monitors. A silent alarm may go off. Everyone knows something about Autism today. "Wasn't there a television show somewhere?"

Radiation from a single Autistic being is enough to alert the crowd. Call it limelight if you want to flatter me. Call it pitiful if you want to feel that sudden spring of human difference. You have options. You read an article and you are wondering wheth-

er my head is mathematical as in the Rain Man movie. You will be surprised. I will not be that mathematical savant you prefer. Mathematics makes me see stars before my eyes.

I can assure you that I have studied every look with the patience of a bone from the other side of the curtain. I know that if I suddenly decided to walk up to you, you will walk away, pretending to unsee me. In your rush, you may forget to hide your startle.

Then I will know I am doing my Autism right!

I may not even be looking at your eyes to know. Yet I sense you are still there behind your curtain not knowing enough. In your belief I would never understand enough.

Seeing Enough...

Rain again! It can rain like a bad habit when it rains in Texas, especially when clouds float in from the gulf.

There was enough rain to cover the window, enough to wash the other side of the world with the color of the curdled sky striped by thick raindrops. Clouds without distinct boundaries, without frame, seemed to blend all over like a smear of sarcasm on the face of shapes and contours. The only prominent shapes outside the window were infinite lines created by whitened raindrops.

You had to look through the rain to see the trees and the houses on the other side; everything else seemed faded and distant; curtained and faded. Trying to outline a shape through rain, isolating the green of a familiar tree and the blue walls of the house across the street, I discovered new movements. That blurred red could be a plastic bag swirling in the puddle. Looking through a window to see blurred shapes is an old habit. Habits are predictable anchors when the other side is blurred.

The sky rained out of a habit formed three days ago, as if a learning pathway, or nervous circuit had been created in its brain and was being reinforced with every determined drop. Habits make a world of difference!

Habit is enough to hold hands with the world, linking the self to its surroundings. That there is a magazine and the magazine needs to be placed in a certain way on the table, that it needs to be held in a certain way.... The gradual ornamentation of details and rituals, locking in the senses and perceptions like an efficient design, is an art to perform and behold! If you haven't seen an Autistic person engaged in ritual, you haven't seen enough! None of your psychological books will describe the details of placing a magazine in a certain way.

Again, if you stop my habit, you will destroy a very valuable piece of curtain that I have woven and learned to see through as I confront the unpredictable world. You are free to look at me through your curtain — as you understand Autism. So let me fix that magazine and show you how to hold it.

Here in Texas, people have a habit. Streets will flow with rain, yet people will tell each other, "We need the rain!" Feeling the need for rain is a habit for Texans, even though one is surrounded by rain.

Everyone needs rain as a habit. No one needs to understand how the water table is going down. Perpetual drought is not a distant future anymore, however faded that reality may look today. Concerned environmentalists warn in their documentaries and United Nation speeches; seeing the inevitable through curtains of warning seems just enough, a kind of comfort. Yet more concrete, more cement continue to widen the width of civilization. Rain on the concrete streets is just a formality. The ground will seek a window to receive the rain. Yet those raindrops will never penetrate through the cement to replenish the over-used ground water.

Civilization has an obsessive habit of expansion. The habit of a handful is to warn each other in Time magazine articles and on PBS specials about acute water shortages. When all around is a wall of doom warnings, we have the thing called awareness, as in Autism awareness. Reality is seen through a curtain of infinite warning. Understanding the now-faded reality through warning leads to a theory. Coal scoops out emptiness in the earth; waterdrops on concrete dry up. You may ignore everything as mere habit.

Habit can also be an acquired interest, to fill an unthinkable void of nothingness that grows branches in the brain. It is not woven out of jest. It is earnest when seen from inside. Habit is absurd when seen from outside.

Autism when seen from inside is just a matter of life; it is earnest. When seen from outside it is a refracting prism, breaking up life into a spectrum of stimulating activities and impulses. You haven't seen enough if you had not seen it inside out.

I have experienced many habits of looking for as long as I can remember. Looking through a glass door reflecting the fan at a doctor's office; looking through my habit in the doctor's eyes, his voice talking through my ears like a melting sound in the twilight, relating those medical terms and instructions — my looking through has its own earnest jest. The boundary between earnestness and jest was dissolved in the blades of the soft hum of the rotating fan that day. That glass door was enough of a boundary between my way of seeing and his way of looking. Did we look enough?

I used to look at a curtain in a wherever place, a semi-transparent laced curtain that would fold the scene outside the window, causing semi-fluid visual images of trees and buildings, color-confused and patterned against the lace design. Sometimes the curtain would slowly swing like a large magical handkerchief at the slightest incoming breeze through the window. Sometimes there would be a flying shape of a bird that would break the continuity of the usual stillness, its edges — a blur of brown or black quickly darting out beyond of the frame of the window.

Outside, sparrows frequented with a kind of certainty in their uncontrolled chirps. You did not have to wait long for the next blurred movement of another bird. There was always a sufficient blur to see.

A semi-fluid world always thickened through those curtains until the sun weakened its glow. My presence was just a formality, unreal as any imagined presence. I was born to memorize a blurred and blended world for all eternity. I have lived behind that curtain long enough to tell.

"Waiting to tell something" is a habit of acquired language. Everyone waits to tell. And no one has time to hear. We are living in an age of human conflict where every word can be heard differently and understood differently. We listen to others' opinions through curtains of our own opinions and beliefs. Language isn't enough to render thoughts transparent. We have blurred meanings when we listen through curtains. No wonder religious texts are interpreted so differently!

Words uttered or read will rush down like rain, projecting themselves out of faces, dropping somewhere on the brief attention span of an audience. My dropping of words in this chapter will eventually evaporate. Millions of words drop out of those television sets and radios every day. Listening through all of those words is our acquired habit.

Looking through an unrushed day at a peopled world is like watching the path of raindrops. Everyone chases time like prowling beasts; their schedules escape like speeding deer, according to the laws of gravity and motion. Seeing through people, isolating a smile from a smile, a frown from the face, reason from an annoying look, can be a full-time job, a job akin to looking out of a curtained window and guessing the blur. Waiting to look at something is also a habit; then, upon finding a sudden outstanding shape, a story begins. Seeing the story through the curtain of visual distraction became a chance, and I began, "Once upon a time through a rain of people I found a shape quite similar to a water faucet."

A story will be enough to hold the view in control. I would view the story by placing a hundred monkeys between me and the story.

There can be hundreds of typewriters with those hundreds of monkeys pushing random keys. One monkey will happen to complete my story by chance. Otherwise the story will wait with its millions of words like everyone waiting to tell. The story may just be an unclear projection seen through the curtain of a million stimuli.

I have lived in a memory of many windows and curtains too long to forget habits. I have lived to see structures appear to fade. I can place that window and the folds of curtains between me and a whole street if the visual impact gets as big as a pile of stubborn stains. I can fade a moving car, blurred outlines disappearing beyond a definite frame covered with a patterned lace. There may be nothing to look at. Sparrows do not show up on streets here. Traffic hyper-sounds its terrific groans through Loop 1 in Austin. Behind the curtain of sound everything will sway like a flat sheet, if one happens to ignore it. And you can feel your own head swing to balance it all up.

Then by chance you will see a blue SUV shape through a mesh of chaotic rush with a white dog looking through the window at you. Window to window, eye to eye. And all the while you waited for this? Between the water faucet and the white dog, in the blue van there was a blank curtain — the cement on the soil. Who knows how many drops of visual impact fell to evaporate.

Scenes will shift like sliding covers from the table and there will be this daisy before your step and you will note its shape in your head. There will always be blank pages in between. Random stories will be the only way to look through and make sense of the vacant lines.

Then you could find one monkey typing your story with a water faucet, a blue van and a white daisy — just by the chance of randomness. That will be enough to tell from behind the curtain.

Fourteen

I once saw half a face in a group photograph on the mantle of a fireplace. I've spent a considerable amount of time creating the other half in my head. I've even placed an imaginary mirror on the edge of the visible part, but the complete face eluded me.

I found it bisected by chance. I had no intention of looking at a photograph of total strangers in someone else's house.

It was a perfect half-afternoon. We'd been invited for lunch, and it was over. I was lingering in the living room where there was a stack of magazines. I like the smell of such stacks.

I had moved close enough to the photograph because the window was reflecting on its glass, and I could see a rocking chair in the reflection outside the window. I like seeing what reflections show. The black-and-white half-centimeter-wide face popped out of the photograph, peeping behind complete faces — like a single fish in water needing to get an unrefracted view of the sun! How do we choose to look if chance has its way? It's pure chance sometimes.

How would you choose to live if chance made you Autistic? The complete life of an Autistic person has a different definition. Here, one has to hold one's own mirror and see through all the myths people talk about.

The surroundings of that half-face were like ripples in a slow motion, frame after frame. They revealed a gradual logic — the systematic erasing of the reflections of the rocking chair, which expanded to the faces of the other members of that group photograph. My task was to complete the other half of the face while the afternoon completed itself.

I can't remember whether I later sat on the rocking chair. I just know that I was completing a task.

The Half-seen

Darkness is a fast-growing ivy. It spreads. Watered with wisdom collected from the day, a drape of darkness draws across your eyes smoothly. Darkness may obscure your vision, but it uncovers tactile memories from the morning.

I had promised myself that morning: I will not touch the door handles of cars. Door handles can surprise you, out of nowhere, with an electrostatic shock. You can feel the electrostatic memory; it moves across the day, even when there isn't any car to look at. Darkness enhances the tactile memory of a metallic door handle.

Although it is still half-dark, you have the assurance that it will soon be completely dark. But you do not yet require electric lights.

The walls look half-relieved to be able to let go of the light that floats down the window, half-sad to let the light fade. Half-lonely windows wait to grow dark around their frames and glass. Reflections will dissolve. There will be nothing waiting outside to look at other than a solitary lamp post. The world of elsewhere fades around the movements within the clock. And at any moment you may actually begin to see clearly glimpses from the day while memorizing the touch of metal on skin. Even the memory of electrostatic touch continues to surprise you. But you may have a ritual to complete by recollecting all those memorable tactile sensitivities you can remember while darkness is semi-lit. Perhaps you may also possess a tactile album where you can see those sensations.

The story of a ritual is a story without a gradual logic.

It is just an ordinary ritual — my staring at darkness — probably grown out of an average idle evening. Certainly something I wouldn't forget performing. I know my neighbor will perform his ritual of going out with his dog, because no one will discover him not picking up after that dog. We all have different rituals linked to half-darkness.

Piled thoughts, messy conclusions of events that one can think about from the day, those meandering streams of ideas over rough and smooth ground inside the world called mind and carrying many washed-away details; regrets and triumphs, their knotted-up mingling can be filtered from a lingering smell of gasoline from that morning's wait at a gas station. All the rest dissolves in a liquid darkness around the clock. Light will be dead; but the throbbing through air will thrive — glimpses from day in the sensation of touch and smell. I like watching dogs, but I would prefer them to smell of magazine pages if they come near me. I prefer them to be smooth as magazine pages when I touch them. I prefer them to be folded and put away when they bark.

Even half a memory of touch can have a voice when colors confuse around the eyes at dusk. A tactile language evolves in its recollection. Recollections move in bones and skin if one has tactile insecurities. When tactile recollections become too sensitive, I turn to a visual memory.

Once, in broad daylight, I watched a monkey in Bangalore — a puzzled look in his eyes — staring at a mirror he was holding with both hands. I do not know how he had acquired it. Probably unsure of what he saw, he held it focused on the sun, it's light reflected upon his face while he continued experimenting, studying, evolving. Was there half a question in his mind? Did the question arise as language? The monkey did not even make a sound! It was quietly studying the mirror.

Then noise came to break that silent concentration, like water filling up a void and emptying out the air. Other monkeys came to have a look. They each proceeded to claim the mirror with disorganized screeches and a ruckus — what an argumentative debacle! Their monkey language filled the stillness. Perhaps the half-question dissolved in the din. What happened to the mirror? I don't know; I didn't see the end. The end could have been a shattering sound: the mirror breaking, spoiling the question. Pieces of the sun under the sky.

Darkness spreads as quickly as ivy, revealing the sound of the monkeys' chatter. The half-darkness echoes all the distant questions that could only be half-answered. Broken moments, piece by piece, join to build up a structure under the eroding light. Did that monkey remember half of its question?

Does anyone know how to join up the jigsaw pieces of Autism and see the overall picture? Or does the real picture erode behind the emphasis of those singled-out blue and solitary puzzle pieces? They taught you to see the pieces and not the picture.

The erosion of thoughts with forgetfulness, floating and shifting around remembered voices, words drizzling, sounds rushing through ravines — conclusions knock as shifting boulders beneath the surface and the trickling sonorous darkness. Everything becomes clear when darkness is still half. You remember your half-looking, half-forgetting to look. You remember looking at someone's shadow when light is half-eroded.

Every time you forget how you must remember his shadow, his shoes, and the stitched folds on his trousers, you forget what he was talking about. Did you actually hear his words or did they fade away like those dreams that you tried to remember? I had isolated his voice from his words. You remember more than half about that shadow. You remember it was hot. A hundred half-thoughts begin, then bubble and pop with a distraction. A half-moon probably waits outside the window. You may see that half a piece of that moon and ignore the darker half. But it will pull the tide all the same.

Unseen chatter of insects thickens as darkness proceeds to win over the other half; each insect loudly alone. You must filter a lingering smell of gasoline out from your memory and concentrate on how effortless loneliness can be.

Often two thoughts appear like actors entering the stage, when darkness is as split as broken thoughts only one personality can emerge at a time. You wait but you can't understand what the actors are supposed to say. Then you begin to actually see "silence" as half-understanding, aggressive enough to cover up all the insect sounds. Darkness is an absolute stage to look into the eyes of silence. All the ticking of time turns out to be absurd movements. The script of muteness is deeper than words. It bears all those incomplete monkey questions. Soon, a solved puzzle picture and unsolved puzzled pieces will look the same.

Darkness grows by half. Sky fades, distance dissolves. It's time to feed on the other senses with visual understanding.

Half-darkness is a half-filled plate of visual gratification.

Fifteen

Advertisements and billboards.

Looking at them makes me memorize a thing or two. I can't just ignore a page-size plea to buy an insurance plan or mattress. Though I never buy anything, I memorize it all the same through repeated looking.

I may ignore a bit of news about the neighborhood — a pet trapped in the closet when it somehow locked the door from the inside, now rescued. I may ignore a bit of news about the recent welfare project adopted by the members of the Rosedale Service Society — they were distributing free blankets to seventeen homeless people with the money they collected. Yet I can't avoid looking at that imposing picture in the biweekly, mid-March issue of the Rosedale Neighbor. *A Kia agent takes up half the page — he's shaking hands with a satisfied customer who stands in front of his new car at the "Capital Kia of Texas" dealership. Even a little KitKat bar looks, in the paper, like the candy Gulliver would sell! Where is your focus? Children can get guitar classes somewhere in the neighborhood, but I under-look that.*

There is always a page or two worth of grocery coupons from a local store for things you don't require.

Advertisements and billboards.

I memorize them without effort. Ask me a science question about Avogadro's hypothesis and I will be attacked with amnesia. Ask me a question about my rituals or tell me to stop smelling magazine pages, and I will be attacked with a second round of amnesia. Did you ask something in ancient Latin? Where is my focus?

Go ahead — you are free to blame my Autism. I can assure you that I remember the details about a very complicated ritual where I will first touch the red backpack and only then will I open the box full of old photographs. At that point I will have time to fix the angles of the magazines on the table — in perfect geometric congruency with the table corners. I don't have to learn theorems to do that! The process is all mapped and highlighted in my head like a billboard. You will never see me doing my rituals wrong — step by step, I follow the rules of the process that I memorized. Shaking hands with everything that makes no reasonable science or sense, I occupy myself with half a page of the day. Can't you see a billboard inside your head? No? (How strange!)

My rituals are always in front of me, outshining everything. I will go through what my day will be like as a ritualistic catalog. Then I will read aloud my evening rituals for a later time. There's no point in reasoning about them. Rituals, like advertisements, glamorize my traits. Otherwise what is life but a page full of news?

Billboards!

Last week I saw two men sticking a giant poster of the Geico Insurance Company on a billboard. I couldn't quite see where they were standing — it was their movement that caught my eye. They looked like two black spiders floating against the white background of the advertisement. The previous advertisement depicted two lawyers from the Bonilla Law Firm whose smiles were smiled chest-deep with professional friendless. (Ignore their fees and pay attention to their smiles.) The billboard was like a stamp on a blue envelope of sky. The new celebrity was a gecko. He was standing with a kind of green dignity: a successful representative of the lizard community, staring down at all the car drivers, a moral reminder. "Ten minutes can save you money...." Pay attention to the money and just ignore the reptile.

Billboard stickers come in bulletin-size and poster-size. Bulletins will dangle by the highway on prominent roads and you will never miss them. Posters will be on arterial roads. This one was the sort of picture one views in a magazine blown up a hundred times. We all love to see the large faces of our movie stars on the big screen. How the smiles and several-feet-long eyebrows on those giant heads move and talk! This animated gecko had a human-like expression. You wonder what a reptilian brain could evolve into if given a chance! You have an obligation to your car to buy insurance.

We have our eyebrows and eyes stuck to our faces highlighting our personalities. I am amazed by the variation in the different ways these stick to faces like stamps so as to represent each and every person. "We are all the same," says democracy, but few become poster people. Others like us — we do the best we can with our looks while helplessly watching the hair designer trim our hair too thin with secret ambition. "Ambition," as Oscar Wilde had defined it, "is the last refuge of failure." Once again our hair style fails our faces. We pay the hair stylist and ignore our faces while we wait for our hair to grow.

The sky, like some kind of a blue wrapping paper, encloses the earth. Pictures of earth from space amaze us. We see this little blue and white blob enveloped by black space. Then we go back to minding what we can manage to mind down here within this package. Where are we getting delivered? We may be shooting out of Hubble telescope from our own air-bubble-wrapped world, but how far will it probe for us? Moon landings no longer excite us. We want to see something big. We can now watch how our war science explodes tiny atoms that blow up big cities right in our living rooms as we shake our heads in horror. Bombs drop like rituals in different cities of the Middle East to be photographed so that we can be appropriately appalled.

When Carl Sagan saw the picture of the "blue dot-like world" taken by Voyager 1 — it was six billion kilometers away from earth — he told Time Magazine, "There is perhaps no better demonstration of the folly of human conceits than this distant image of our tiny world." I have seen messages on billboards — "Let's make earth a better place!"

Who will initiate this folly?

2,500 years ago, Aesop knew about such folly. One fable talks about a mouse-meeting where the mice decide how to caution each other about a cat. They decide to tie a bell around the cat's neck so that whenever the cat comes close, the bell will ring to warn them. However, none of the mice actually bothered to tie the bell around a living breathing cat. Who will initiate any of those slogans they put on the billboard?

It is so easy to warn each other about the state of the world. Many people seem to know exactly what to do. A billboard I once encountered advised all the gas-guzzling, smoke-oozing trucks and cars to take good care of the earth! Every truck had an attitude of "dare me" at the warning.

Cities get makeovers. It is more than your mere haircut. When Rio was chosen as the Olympic city, the authorities directed an ambitious makeover of the city. An Olympic Villages was constructed, new roads were built, politics were hushed, and no political demonstrations were allowed… and still the Australian team refused to move into the Olympic Village! It wasn't clean enough for their standards.

Games and competitions masked political protests. Striving for gold kept the spirits high. However small an individual moment may be, the winning moment is big. Many stories about the winner's medal were presented. Years of sweat compressed in a medal!

"Mama exhorted her children at every opportunity to 'jump at the sun.' We might not land on the sun, but at least we would get off the ground." So says folklorist and novelist Zora Neale Hurston in her novel *Dust Tracks on a Road*. Big stories to inspire a piece of shining gold. Big messages to write on the billboard.

That blue dot that Carl Sagan saw does indeed hide human efforts and conceits if looked at from space. Big news coverage of the Rio Olympics, and no one was talking about the South African blade runner scandal from the previous London Olympics. Everyone moves on — one medal moment to other medal moments. The earth moves on, covering 583 million miles in one year! Memories and moments are left behind; we move on, from billboard to billboard, message to message. Some of us memorize them — how two lawyers were erased by a green gecko. Who bought the lawyers out?

The things that show up; it's a mere second before the next thing shows up. What are we forcing our eyes to see?

Once, six or seven or maybe seven and half years ago, I happened to see a heavy red backpack on someone's narrow shoulders. I don't know who the bearer of those shoulders was, but that heavy red backpack with shoulders was included in a list of things I saw. I kept the visual image inside of my head where much important information could have been stored. We can pluck visual pictures, scavenging the streets of our encounters and load up our heads. For a while I carried the image of the narrow shoulders carrying a red backpack and all its heaviness like a portable billboard, squeezing it in my brain. And after that it all began to happen.

My curious mind began to wonder what was inside the backpack some five days later. Nothing I could fill it with would satisfy me. I began to open the backpacks of people at school just to get an idea of what might be in there. It had been so prominently placed in my head. Of course, one can always get away with things if one is chronically

Autistic, including opening other people's backpacks. But you mustn't worry about *your* backpack. I abandoned the backpack habit long ago while the earth was six or seven or maybe seven and a half years younger, seven times 583 million miles ago, working its way in a closed elliptical circuit, a solitary runner with no finishing line. All that practice of racing through eons and no medal moment for the earth.

New questions arise — Do cats catch mice any more or do modern and updated cats prefer pre-cooked high-protein cat food from Rachel Ray?

Images pile up. Some images become the highlights of life like that of a broken mirror. Someone had placed a large mirror on Poinsettia Avenue in Los Angeles on the curb to be disposed of. It was as large as a door! It had slit the world along its diagonal into two. A probable world — broken trees, broken people, and broken thoughts that could exist if it existed behind it — began to pile up inside my head. Mind, I find, is always better than Stomach. After a meal the stomach is filled. But when the mind eats up an image the outgrowth and branches can touch infinity. That broken mirror dissecting the world grew big as a billboard in my head. Then it grew further to churn out galaxies of visual possibilities. Will someone take it to space and look at a divided world?

The size of the Milky Way is measured in time: 120,000 light years in diameter. And there are some 400 billion stars that have churned out of the center, to turn it around 630 kilometers per second. We on earth take up a tiny space in it. Who would have the eyes to see the enormous image in space? The galaxy moves between bigger billboards along that terrific highway of a terrific town called universe that we will never understand in our lifetime.

When that scientist chopped his living specimen of a sponge into really tiny pieces in his dish, and left the room to return after a while, he found that those tiny pieces had rearranged themselves into hundreds of miniature beings identical to the parent sponge.

We carry the Milky Way-sized data in our sponge-like minds; piece by piece, image by image, it begins to collect. Using the data, we are able to imagine an alien ship, dream the impossible. Because of the data in our heads, we can grow the face of God. We know how important a face is. Once I had tried to search for the face of a snail in a picture.

One day a snail can touch the toe of a man showing him the miniature image of the Milky Way in his logarithmic spiral shell. But man will ignore the snail. He will continue to wait for the Hubble images to memorize him.

Afterword

I had set forth to enjoy the weather, inhaling the changing colors of the leaves. My eyes were my headlights, showing me the way. The chilled air tickled my nostrils. Texas was cooling and cooling fast that October morning. Like a metallic conductor, it heated or cooled with the slightest provocation from the tilting and turning earth. We were celebrating outside after a very hot spell of summer. Then came Hurricane Harvey! Now every morning felt like a mandatory clean up. The wind and rain seemed to be medicated after a manic seizure.

While I was walking along the familiar trail, I stepped across a bright yellow jacket, under which the head of a squirrel appeared and disappeared, playing peekaboo. I couldn't figure out why someone would discard such a jacket, which was new, that far out on the trail — why they would let a squirrel take possession of it? There are so many things we expect to see and then there are others that surprise us. The jacket and the busy squirrel made an interesting island on the trail. All around them were knotted grasses and weeds, woven in a disorderly manner, matted with mud.

Knotted weeds always look like a complicated economics. The yellow jacket lay there like a simplified project and the squirrel was the sole explorer. He had solved the economics of knots and reduced everything into a simplified system that worked for him. He knew what he was looking at. Many of us continue to search all our lives for the particular thing we should look at.

There is so much to look at! You open your eyes in the morning and begin to look. Where is the new packet of shaving blades? You have seen enough and before it is nine o'clock you have looked through the garbage and still have not found the new packet of blades. You will be seeing more! Why is the magazine on the kitchen shelf when it's not supposed to be there? You will see things out of place if you are bothered by them. Everything in this world turns upside down and out of place during the day. You can be a squirrel discovering a yellow jacket on a path in the puzzling economics of life. And you can find what to look at like the squirrel and ignore the rest.

Long ago a primitive human being gazed up at the yellow orb in the sky and grunted out the sound "sun." They who heard the word grunted out "sun" in unison, because the first grunt of the word was from the leader of their tribe whom they all revered. The sun was something that can't be out of place. Then they told their children what to call that yellow orb, even if they wanted to call it more than a mere substance. Slowly, the next generation called the yellow light in the sky "sun." They attached other things they saw to different sounds and soon they began to see the sounds they uttered — for when we hear the sound "sun" we cannot unsee the shape. We cannot unsee the light and we cannot unfeel the heat. The mind of the squirrel could feel the warmth under the jacket. He did not bother to label it by any name and complicate the simple pleasures of the autumn morning. The economics of complexity are a choice.

How complicated can we make our visual experience? As children, we learn the latitudes that ring the earth; against those latitudes the westerlies and trade winds arrowing this way and that with the explanations of the Coriolis effect. One day, we outgrow the knowledge to find the simple pleasures of the wind on our face during a morning walk. And then we are asked to focus on the yellow jacket of a hurricane. Talk about out of place! The Weather Channel zeroes in on Harvey the way Harvey zeroes in on the Gulf Coast. A simple drive to the grocery store is forbidden. Between you and the store is a flash flood waiting to get you. Does anyone wonder what squirrels do when wind attacks their trees? On what do birds and squirrels focus in that movement?

What forces us to focus when we have to jump on the platform from a moving train? Once in a station in Chennai, mother and I had to focus. Rushing to catch our train, we got up on the wrong train in the rush, because the train from Bangalore to Chennai had delayed us. We were catching the train to Howrah at Chennai. The time of the wrong train coincided with the train we were supposed to be on. We realized the mistake only when the wrong train we were on began to move. There was nothing to reason as I saw mother, in the blink of a moment, desperately throwing our suitcases onto the platform. She was then grabbing my hand to jump out — the next blink of the moment. I saw the ground moving further behind the train before the jump — that's where the force of focus was that day. I believe I was nine. That day time was perceived as a series of blinks. When we talk about it today, the moment seemed complicated, and yet we focused.

I couldn't have known that one day I would be walking on an American trail, learning to look at a squirrel under a discarded jacket, and wiling away the time.

What if the human and the squirrel exchanged places? His head popped in and out, teasing all of the theories that never matter. The complex world of information continues to weave and grow heavy with facts. All our lives we are gathering the garbage of facts to make sense of what we see. Touring NASA in Houston, I gathered a book with facts collected by the touring astronauts — every page was factual with the pictures they took.

One day, I could be dropping in on a desert to meet the Little Prince from the book by Antoine de Saint-Exupéry. And I will tell him what I learned from all of this seeing — "We are squirrels under the jacket called sky."